Space
to Imagine

Study Creative Writing at Bath Spa

The Creative Writing Centre at Bath Spa University has been helping people get published for over three decades. We are now accepting applications for Autumn 2012 entry onto the following programmes of study:

MA Creative Writing

MA Writing for Young People

MA Scriptwriting

MA in Travel & Nature Writing

PhD in Creative Writing

www.bathspa.ac.uk/schools/humanities-and-cultural-industries/creative-writing

GRANTA

12 Addison Avenue, London W11 4QR
email editorial@granta.com
To subscribe go to www.granta.com
Or call 845-267-3031 (toll-free 866-438-6150) in the United States, 020 8955 7011 in the United Kingdom

ISSUE 117: AUTUMN 2011

EDITOR	John Freeman
DEPUTY EDITOR	Ellah Allfrey
ARTISTIC DIRECTOR	Michael Salu
ASSISTANT EDITOR	Patrick Ryan
ONLINE EDITOR	Ted Hodgkinson
EDITORIAL ASSISTANT	Yuka Igarashi
PUBLICITY	Saskia Vogel
ASSISTANT DESIGNER	Daniela Silva
FINANCE	Geoffrey Gordon, Morgan Graver, Craig Nicholson
MARKETING AND SUBSCRIPTIONS	David Robinson
SALES DIRECTOR	Brigid Macleod
SALES MANAGER	Sharon Murphy
TO ADVERTISE CONTACT	Kate Rochester, katerochester@granta.com
IT MANAGER	Mark Williams
PRODUCTION ASSOCIATE	Sarah Wasley
PROOFS	John English, Katherine Fry, Kelly Falconer, Vimbai Shire
PUBLISHER	Sigrid Rausing
CONTRIBUTING EDITORS	Daniel Alarcón, Diana Athill, Peter Carey, Sophie Harrison, Isabel Hilton, Blake Morrison, John Ryle, Lucretia Stewart, Edmund White

For Sam R., whose idea this was

In the United States, *Granta* is published in association with Grove/Atlantic Inc., 841 Broadway, 4th Floor, New York, NY 10003, and distributed by PGW. All editorial queries should be addressed to the London office.

Granta USPS 000-508 is published four times per year (February, May, August and November) by *Granta*, 12 Addison Avenue, London W11 4QR, United Kingdom, at the annual subscription rate of £34.95 and $45.99.

Airfreight and mailing in the USA by Agent named Air Business, c/o Worldnet Shipping USA Inc., 149–35 177th Street, Jamaica, New York, NY 11434. Periodicals postage paid at Jamaica, NY 11431.

US POSTMASTER: Send address changes to *Granta*, PO Box 359, Congers, NY 10920-0359.

Granta is printed and bound in Italy by Legoprint. This magazine is printed on paper that fulfils the criteria for 'Paper for permanent document' according to ISO 9706 and the American Library Standard ANSI/NIZO Z39.48-1992 and has been certified by the Forest Stewardship Council (FSC). *Granta* is indexed in the American Humanities Index.

ISBN 978-1-905881-36-9

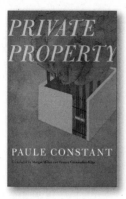
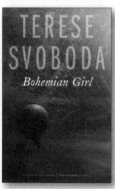
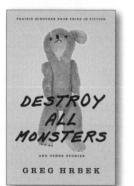

DISCOVER THE WRITER'S LIFE IN NEW YORK CITY

CREATIVE WRITING AT THE NEW SCHOOL

Master of Fine Arts in Creative Writing

Concentrations in fiction, poetry, nonfiction, and writing for children. Fellowships and financial aid available.

Bachelor's Program in the Liberal Arts

Writing students seeking a BA may apply to the Riggio Honors Program. Accepted students are eligible for partial scholarships.

The Riggio Honors Program is offered in conjunction with the Leonard and Louise Riggio Writing & Democracy Initiative at the New School.

**2011–2012
Director: Robert Polito
Associate Director: Jackson Taylor
Associate Chair: Luis Jaramillo**

MFA FACULTY
Jeffery Renard Allen, Robert Antoni, Catherine Barnett, Susan Bell, Mark Bibbins, Susan Cheever, Jonathan Dee, Elaine Equi, Jennifer Michael Hecht, Ann Hood, Shelley Jackson, Zia Jaffrey, Hettie Jones, James Lasdun, David Lehman, Suzannah Lessard, David Levithan, Phillip Lopate, Patrick McGrath, Honor Moore, Sigrid Nunez, Dale Peck, Darryl Pinckney, Robert Polito, Jenni Quilter, Helen Schulman, Tor Seidler, Laurie Sheck, Darcey Steinke, Benjamin Taylor, Jackson Taylor, Craig Teicher, Susan Van Metre, Sarah Weeks, Brenda Wineapple, Stephen Wright, Tiphanie Yanique

MFA VISITING FACULTY
Max Blagg, Deborah Brodie, Patricia Carlin, Rosemary Deen, Marilyn Goldin, Vivian Gornick, Gary Indiana, Dave Johnson, Joyce Johnson, Mary Lee Kortes, Wendy Lesser, Greil Marcus, Sharon Mesmer, Flaminia Ocampo, Marie Ponsot, David Prete, John Reed, Lloyd Schwartz, Susan Shapiro, Justin Taylor, Frederic Tuten, Victoria Wilson

RIGGIO HONORS PROGRAM FACULTY
Jeffery Renard Allen, Catherine Barnett, Mark Bibbins, Patricia Carlin, Elizabeth Gaffney, Tim Griffin, Tom Healy, Zia Jaffrey, Suzannah Lessard, Sigrid Nunez, Greil Marcus, René Steinke, Sam Tanenhaus, Lynne Tillman, Linda Tvrdy, Tiphanie Yanique

www.newschool.edu/writing3

CONTENTS

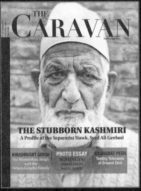

GRANTA

FALSE BLOOD

Will Self

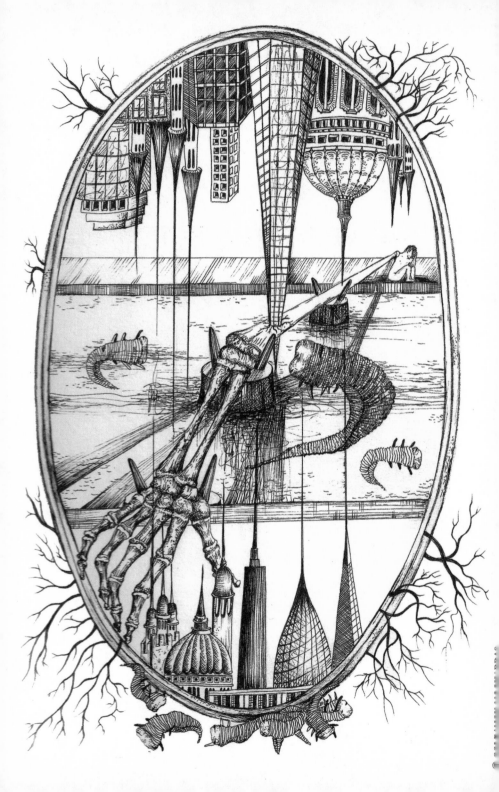

Sometime over the winter of 2010–11 I began to be gorged with blood – or, rather, my blood itself began to be gorged with red blood cells, with haemoglobin. I didn't pay it much attention – mostly because I didn't realize it was happening, the only perceptible symptoms being a certain livid tinge to my face and to my hands, which, I joked to family and friends, had started to resemble those pink Marigold washing-up gloves. When I took my gorged hands out of my jeans pockets the tight denim hems left equally vivid bands smeared across their backs – these, I facetiously observed, were the colour of those yellow Marigold washing-up gloves.

I had no intention of doing anything about my pink-and-yellow-striped hands. This is not, I stress, because I'm especially neglectful of my health – at times I can verge on hypochondria – but rather because they didn't strike me as obviously cancerous. I was on the lookout for the crab – but then I always am. It scuttled away my father and mother, the latter at sixty-five, an age she would've described herself – also facetiously – as 'getting younger'. And during the preceding year it had been nipping at my forty-seven-year-old wife, trying to drag her down the sable strand and into the salt, chill waters that lap against life. She had been diagnosed with breast cancer in June of 2010, had a mastectomy in August, followed by a gruelling autumn then winter of chemotherapy and a silent spring of radiation.

My wife bore her illness in a manner that demanded nothing but admiration. As we walked down the grotty staircase of Guy's Hospital Tower from the consultation where she'd been informed of how radical her surgery would need to be, she turned to me and said, 'I'm so lucky. If it was twenty-five years ago, or I was somewhere else in the world, I'd've just received a death sentence.' I imagined that if they had cut out her heart instead of cutting off her breast they would have found 'devoid of self-pity' written on it. I was less sanguine – metaphorically speaking. I felt distracted and doomy; I was a dilatory carer – and at times seemingly wilfully inept. I could just about manage the basics: the feeding and dressing of our two younger children, and the forcing upon her of increasingly unwanted cups of tea.

It didn't help that we seemed to be at the epicentre of a cancer cluster: one friend was dying of leukaemia in the Hammersmith Hospital, another was in the process of being diagnosed – a third had had half his throat and jaw chopped out. Cancer? I hear you ask. Yes, of course it was fucking cancer, what else could it be? I fully expected cancer myself. To paraphrase the late and greatly pathetic roué Willie Donaldson, you cannot live as I have and not end up with cancer. There was the genetic factor to begin with, and then there's been the toxic landscape of carcinogens – the yards of liquor, the sooty furlongs left behind by chased heroin, the miles driven and limped for over a decade to score crack which then scoured its way into my lungs. The prosaically giant haystacks of Virginia tobacco hardly bear mentioning – being, in contrast, merely bucolic.

No, I was on the lookout for the crab – not a pair of lobster's claws. It was my wife who eventually sent me across the road to the GP, a shrewdly downbeat practitioner who in the past had declined to check my cholesterol levels (no need, you've cut your smoking right back, you're thin and fit, and your blood pressure's low) or send me for a prostate-cancer biopsy (too many false negatives so there's hardly any point), but now took one look at the human-into-crustacean transmogrification and sent me straight down to St Thomas's for a blood test. The results came within a couple of days, and when I saw him in person he confirmed what he'd told me over the phone: 'Your haemoglobin is right up, and your white blood cell count is also elevated. I can't be certain but I think there's a strong possibility it's –'

I pre-empted him: 'Polycythaemia vera?'

'Aha,' he said. 'Been googling, have you?' I conceded that I had.

'Well,' he continued, 'the Wiki entries are pretty thoroughly vetted – if you stick to that you're on safe ground.'

I inwardly congratulated myself for having done just that. But still, polycythaemia vera – what was *that*? A disease that sounded like a Greek goddess spliced with an East End pub landlady, a disease that resulted from a single gene mutating and instructing your bone marrow to indulge in a mindless overproduction of red blood cells. A disease that was rare, chronic, incurable and, while no one yet understood the exact reasons for the mutagenesis, disproportionately present among Ashkenazi Jews. I liked that – in my transgenerationally facetious way: my mother had passed a generous dose of Jewish anti-Semitism down to me, and along with it this Jewish disease had been bred in the bone.

My blasé general practitioner sent me on my way. I had to go to the Ukraine on a journalistic assignment – was it all right to fly, what with my thickened blood and the consequent increased risk of stroke, heart attack or deep-vein thrombosis? 'Oh, yes.' He airily waved a papery hand. 'People don't get DVT from flying – they get it from sitting still. Just make sure you keep moving.'

When my wife was having her operation the windows of her surgical ward at St Thomas's looked out over the imperious clutter of central London jumbled in the bends of the Thames – its giant Ferris wheel and hypertrophied concrete bunker of a theatre, its recently whitened kingly sepulchre and its admiral-tipped bodkin. When my friend was having half his tongue and throat chopped out at University College Hospital, I went to visit him and found he had a still more spectacular view: south-facing from the Euston Road, the grid-pattern of Bloomsbury and Marylebone seaming into the hugger-mugger from which spears Senate House and Centrepoint. Further off sprouted the thicket of the City, while the North Downs smeared greenly along the horizon.

It occurred to me then that, for a Londoner, serious illness often afforded this curious discombobulation as one became a tourist in one's own city, resident for a week or two in a subsidized hostel conveniently located for all the visitor attractions. And so, as I rose up from the bowels of London Bridge Tube station, en route to my first hospital appointment, I toyed with the idea of turning left and heading for the London Dungeon instead of right to the Guy's Haematology Day Unit. I'd never bothered to visit the Dungeon before – but its cheesy tableaux of caged, flayed and beheaded dummy felons spattered with ersatz gore would probably be a nice distraction from the far more veridical Guignol that awaited me.

Tunnelling out from the station to ground level I found myself in St Thomas Street hard against the soaring glassy flank of the Shard, the city's latest indulgence in postmodernist desktop-toy ornamentation. Its starchitect, Renzo Piano, has spoken of how, when completed, the eighty-seven-storey building – the European Union's highest – will appear altogether insubstantial, tapering away into expressive angles of glazing within which the cityscape will be reflected. But I could apprehend nothing of this nothingness – in my current state the Shard was notable only for being acuminate: a vast hypodermic needle lancing up into the cloudy tissue of the sky.

I've never really understood those who can read a lot of poetry – to do so would be akin to overdosing on metaphoric truffles, so rich is this semiotic food. First encountered in my twenties, Roethke's 'Dolor' has sated me for half a lifetime, and I regurgitated yet again as I mounted the iron stairs to the second-floor entrance of the hospital's Southwark Wing: 'Desolation in immaculate public places / Lonely reception room, lavatory, switchboard, / The unalterable pathos of basin and pitcher . . .' Is this not, I mused, the real horror of the affluent West? Its shameless juxtaposition of the mass repetition with the individual sickening. 'And I have seen dust from the walls of institutions / Finer than flour, alive, more dangerous than silica . . .' The sign above a door read SPIRITUAL CARE, but a steel shutter had been rolled over it, and through a hole in this I could see a combination lock.

On the stairs there was a taped-up piece of A4 paper advising me to go up and down them for ten minutes a day if I wanted to maintain good CARDIAC HEALTH. Elsewhere in the corridors other notices signposted DOMESTIC WASTE or alerted to upcoming events such as TRACHEOTOMY STUDY DAY. At the fourth floor I could turn left to the BLOOD BANK, or right to HAEMATOLOGY 2. In front of me, piled together with cardboard boxes and abandoned computer equipment on the filmy-beige linoleum tiling were some nylon bags about eighteen inches cubed – white ones were labelled 'Buffy Coats'; red ones 'Platelets'. This was the realm of the logical positivists, I thought; every object comes provided with its own caption so meaning is implicit. I had trafficked in disease as a metaphor for twenty years now, grafting the defining criteria of pathologies – their aetiology, their symptoms, their prognoses and their outcomes – on to phenomena as diverse as the human psyche and the urban fabric, yet now I had a disease that seemed to me to *be* a metaphor – although of what exactly I couldn't yet divine – I found myself in a viscid substrate, cultured with rapidly multiplying literalisms.

When I told friends about my condition and what the most effective therapy for it was they all – all! – said the same thing: What? You have to get *bled*? What will they do that with? Leeches? I found this stereotypy infuriating and wondered what its cause could be. Was it that buried beneath a thin skin of acquired medical know-how there lay the heart of Galen beating in black bile? Or was it simply that they'd heard leeches were once again being used in some contemporary procedures and wanted to show they were au fait? I applied the cigarette end of my contempt to my friends' imagined leeches. How big a leech would be required, I spat at them, given that they've got to take two pints a week out of me? No, they use a needle – and a big one, since my blood is currently as thick as tomato purée.

This silenced them. But then nobody talks about therapeutic bleeding much, although it transpired that a neighbour of mine – tall, eccentric, with the carelessly drawn appearance of a Quentin Blake children's illustration – was also having his blood regularly siphoned off. I encountered him outside his double-fronted and unrendered

house, and he jollily recounted how his haemochromatosis meant he
had to have a pint taken out every now and then. 'I've got a friend at
King's,' he said, 'who does it in a broom cupboard for me – not strictly
allowed, but there you go. Anyway, he lets me take the blood away with
me so I can put it on my pumpkins.' He gestured to his front steps,
where every autumn a gaggle of the engorged and vampiric gourds
clustered. 'It really is the most excellent fertilizer.' This Addams
Family domesticity was cheering – and I could understand why my
neighbour's pumpkins thrived on his blood, given that his condition
meant it was iron-enriched. But what conceivable use would I find for
my own rubicund brew?

On at least four of the sixteen occasions between April and July
that I went to Guy's for my venesections I was accosted outside the
McDonald's on St Thomas Street by the same young man. He was
well spoken if shabbily dressed, and had the limp-scrape gait and the
paradoxical features – at once sharply etched and poorly registered
– of the street junky. Each time he asked me for change and each
time I asked him if he had a drug problem. The first time he denied
this I told him: 'Sorry, I only give money to people who have a drug
problem.' So, predictably, he back-pedalled: 'No, no, I do have
an 'abit . . .' addiction being such a great leveller it planes away even
the ability to detect irony. Then I zeroed in for the kill. 'I'm sorry again,
but I don't give money to liars.' And he desperately rejoined, 'I juss
don't like to admit it straight up. Y'know what people are like . . .' Finally,
I relented and gave him a pound coin or two, before subjecting him
– in the time-honoured Sally Army way – to a homily in return for
his handout.

I told him how I too had once been where he was: a heroin addict
– on and off for twenty years – but that I had been clean now for
almost twelve. I told him that if he wanted to get clean and stay
that way all he had to do was follow some remarkably simple steps,
the first of which was to make the admission that he was indeed
an addict, rather than lying about it to himself and the world. Of
course, the second time I saw the junky he recognized me halfway

through the exchange and the third time we chatted away like old acquaintances about all the insuperable barriers there were to his taking my blindingly simple advice. The fourth time I saw him I just handed him the money – I was tiring of the charade, both his and mine.

I first stuck a needle in my arm in the summer of 1979 – I was seventeen years old. I often think back with a protective tenderness towards my younger self and wish I were somehow able to dissuade him from such a mutilation, from breaking the blood-air barrier in that crazy way. Sometimes, when I hear people without experience of addiction blame addicts for their behaviour I feel like saying to them: You simply don't understand – how can a *child* be held responsible for doing such a dreadful thing to himself? But then again, at other times I have to acknowledge: it was done wilfully. No matter how obscured they were by the fogs of adolescent self-deception, I was fully acquainted with the facts.

My concern here isn't with addiction to drugs – although that horror has cast a long shadow over my life and the lives of my family, and infiltrated my fictive inscape, poisoning its field margins, salting its earth. No, my concern is with addiction to needles. The addiction to transfusing solutions of heroin, or cocaine, or amphetamine into my own blood was anterior – but the obsession with the hypodermic and the compulsion to drive it home followed with inexorably maddening logic. I was never good at shooting up – a deranging oxymoron if ever there was one. In a way, I think this was deliberate: to be inefficient at it was another form of denying that I was really an addict, akin to never having a methadone prescription, or shoplifting. I taught myself to do it, and quickly transformed my skinny arms into an appliqué of scabs, sores, blotches and welts. I have never been good at DIY. To give herself an effective hit, the drug user must apply a tourniquet, raise a vein, probe with the needle, neatly pierce the epidermis and the wall of the vein, watch for the smoky plume of blood to rise up through the needle and into the barrel of the syringe, release the tourniquet then push the plunger home.

A practised self-injector will slightly depress the plunger of the hypodermic, then deftly pull it a little way out, depress it a bit more, pull it out again – in so doing the barrel will become suffused with blood, while the inrush of the drugs takes place with a mounting rhythm of successive waves. In the bankrupt trade of self-annihilation (CLOSING DOWN SALE – ALL SCRUPLES MUST GO!), this technique is known as 'flushing the works', and some habitués compare its effects to the gathering tempo of an orgasm – especially when the solution in the syringe is compounded of heroin and cocaine, a so-called 'speedball'. I last shot a speedball in the summer of 1992 – and, indeed, I think that may well have been the last time I ever injected drugs at all; at any rate I have no memory of doing it thereafter. In part I stopped because I'd had a period off drugs altogether in the late eighties and, although I was sliding headlong back into addiction, I knew that this practice was giving it a shot in the arm – metaphorically speaking. But I also desisted because by then the laborious home chemistry of freebasing cocaine – my favoured snuffle – had given way to the prêt-à-porter of crack, and this was quite as speedily an effective drug-delivery system.

What matter, the facts are these: for a decade or so I stuck needles in my arms, my hands, my feet and on one particularly weird occasion my penis. I schlepped across town in all weathers to buy needles and syringes from Halls off Shaftesbury Avenue, or the aptly named Bliss Chemist's, which had branches at Marble Arch and on Willesden Lane – because these were the only outlets in London that sold them over the counter, no questions asked. For a junky who was bad at shooting up I was peculiarly fastidious. I knew all about the risks – from septicaemia to 'dirty hits' (when bacteria are injected along with drugs), and viruses such as hepatitis B – initially – then latterly hep C and HIV. I took precautions to guard against these maladies, such as using sterile needles wherever possible, and if I couldn't, cleaning the old 'works' with bleach in solution. Most fortuitously I hardly ever shared needles – indeed, I can only remember doing this on two or perhaps three occasions, but it's significant that one of these involved the flea's progress of the syringe. 'It suck'd me first, and now sucks thee / And in this flea our two bloods mingled be . . .' – between two fellow addicts – both of whom subsequently turned out to have hepatitis C – then on to me.

I was lucky. HIV is comparatively feeble anyway – although intravenous drug use remains a royal road for its progress – but hepatitis C was, is and always will be a devilish shape-shifter of a virus: tough, long-lived, ever-mutating. A grapeshot of these virions cut a broad swathe through my generation of IV drug users, so broad that to be hep C-free is almost the exception. I was lucky – I had spent long nights shooting cocaine every fifteen minutes or so until my arms were as luridly wounded as those of a persecuted medieval saint. I had poised with a syringe full of coke stuck in my arm for long, heart-thudding moments, conscious that if I depressed the plunger I'd have a heart attack or a stroke. I had become so fixated on this perversion of medical therapeutics that I found myself on several occasions, when I didn't have the wherewithal, boiling up the old bits of cigarette filter through which the scuzzy drugs had been drawn off, mixing this sub-strength potion with citric acid (used to facilitate the dissolving of the browner, less refined form of heroin), then shooting this up. A process I repeated several times over until I was injecting more or less pure citric acid which burned bitterly through my traumatized veins.

I shot up and up and up and up . . . then fell back to earth, and was left with nothing more troubling than fading external track marks and thrombosis around the veins I had used most frequently. Not for me the arterial groin-shot gone wrong that leads to amputation – or the Christiane F.-style neck shot that leads, presumably, to decapitation. Old junkies spoke of the fine deposits left by repeated injections at the top of the heart that years later descended – 'Finer than flour, alive, more dangerous than silica . . .' – stopping the clockwork for good, but this I doubted.

Of course, there was something else troubling me – shame. And it troubled me more the further I got away from the needles and drugs and the whole senseless go-round of addiction. When you're an IV drug user you are so way out beyond the pale that your malaise becomes entangled with the caduceus: you depend on doctors as much as you revile them – and you believe they owe you their health-giving expertise free and on demand. But as I got well I began to see my body as the carelessly used property of the National Health Service – damaged goods I would do best to hide away.

There was this, and there was the phobia. I suspect that all those who've put needles behind them have to develop a loathing of them, have to reinforce their repudiation with the horror that was formerly swept aside by insensate desire. I couldn't bear to look at an injection being administered on the television – let alone live. I recoiled from all pointy things – and from the red gush they dug in human soil. Even walking along the street the spear-tipped railings caught and tore at my eye. If I saw a motorcycle speeding through the London traffic, on its white top box the life-saving legend HUMAN BLOOD, I recoiled. My blood may not have been infected – but it was tainted. When I had to have a blood test for this or that suspected ailment, I became tense: I would have to tell the nurse about my past or else they would try to pierce the still-thrombotic veins – and then he or she would become tense, and then it would all go wrong. So wrong.

Sitting in the consulting room of the haematologist at Guy's, I heard little of what she said. She was a serious head girl with straight eyebrows and a crisp white coat – I was a shabby delinquent. Or rather, I listened to what she said but didn't register its full implications. At the time I thought this was because although I'd given out the strong message that I didn't wish to be patronized or spoken down to, the reality was that she was speaking way over my untutored head – and, besides, no one *really* wants to know what's going on in their bone marrow. Whether you consult a physician whose opinions are adamantine, so coated have they been in the hardest of science, or a shaman whose magical operations have been orally transmitted for time out of mind, the patient's requirement is for expertise, while all we have to divvy up in return for this is our faith.

When I asked about prognosis she was circumspect in the way good practitioners are – after all, statistics are only applicable to groups, not individuals. 'I have some patients,' she said, 'who I've maintained purely on venesections for ten to fifteen years.' Later – much later – the 'some' came back to me, but in the short term there were those venesections to cope with: a tourniquet would have to be applied, a vein found, a needle stuck through dermis and vascular wall . . . and then, no payback, no flushed warm gush of lotus juice or essence of Lethe, only the siphoning of my deathly blood. I listened to what the consultant said about red cell counts and white cell counts and platelets but these were only so many cubic nylon bags jumbled in the corridors of my mind; I *heard* her when she said the venesections – the beginning of a lifetime on the needle – needed to begin right away, that morning, at once. Now.

In the Day Unit the dark vinyl chairs tip back at the press of a button and small footrests simultaneously emerge. If it weren't for the way the chairs are arranged in groups, or the fact that the ministering staff wear a variety of unflattering uniforms, I thought, this might be the business-class section of some wide-bodied jet bumbling down to Heathrow along a dangerously low-altitude flight path. After all, here through the long strip of windows were the unrivalled views of central London landmarks – Tate Modern, St Paul's Cathedral, assorted other Wren churches – that I had come to expect from medical tourism. The only problem was me. I saw spires, lightning rods, phone masts, pylons – an acicular world upon the myriad sharpened points of which I was poised, petrified, lest the slightest movement see me espaliered.

It was worse than pathetic of me to be so squeamish – all around me on the unit sat my peers, my blood brothers and sisters with their haemochromatosis and their polycythaemia vera, their sickle-cell anaemia – and worse. Some hid their baldness with hats or makeshift moabs, others had exposed flesh that was empurpled by lesions; all of them appeared utterly indifferent to the cannulae stuck in their arms or the backs of their hands. They read magazines or fingered laptops, drowsed between headphones or chatted with friends and relatives, all pointedly ignoring the transparent bags of factor-this or factor-that being factored into them, that hung from stands by their shoulders.

A nurse had to talk me through that first venesection as I gurned and contorted. I directed her away from the veins she favoured in the pits of my elbows because I knew these had thrombosis, and denied her access to the ones that twisted, ivy-like, around the back of the forearm, because I also knew – in junky parlance – that they were 'rollers' which would worm away from the needle. The needle was, of necessity, thick – and it took a long time for her to get it inside me. But my blood was thicker still – and it took a long time to pulse out of me. To begin with, the staff were perfectly accommodating and they put me on one of the available beds, such was my nervousness; however, by the time I got to my third venesection they were chivvying me towards the business-class section. Here, a nurse infected by my own tension collapsed a vein on one arm, then, on the other arm, failed to bind the needle into the vein so that it shot out with a gush of blood. Over the following twenty-four hours the bruises streaked like sepsis. When I returned to the unit for the next venesection I was back in one of the bays, back on one of the beds. Here, distraught, I confessed to the trained vampire in her cotton cloak who was having difficulty dowsing for a suitable vein that I had once been an intravenous drug user.

Was it my imagination, or did the attitude towards me on the unit change after this? Was there a certain chilliness engendered in the stuffily antiseptic atmosphere? Before my next appointment with the haematologist, when the phlebotomist was trying to get a blood sample, I fainted and became the cynosure for a bustle of activity: wheelchaired into the Day Unit and hefted onto a bed, the sensors of an electrocardiogram machine were strapped onto me. I was visited by an impossibly beautiful registrar who, like all the staff, called me by my given name – William – while she held my wrist and peered down with unfeigned enthusiasm into my eyes. William – no one had called me that since childhood, no one except patronising police reading my identity off my driving licence. It occurred to me that it was this that made it so difficult for me to divine the metaphoric import of my condition – for how could a child be expected to understand such a thing?

Two pints a week, eight pints a month – in a couple of months a whole me's worth of blood would be decanted into plastic carafes and laid down, possibly in one of the cubic nylon bags in the corridor. London junky and criminal slang for blood is claret, but this was a joyless *vendage* and a useless vintage fit only for disposal. Still I de-trained in the bowels of London Bridge, still I dragged myself past the glassy haunches of the Shard, which, even as I was draining away, grew taller and more pointed. Still I passed the permanently shuttered door to SPIRITUAL CARE, still I mounted the stairs and passed along the corridor. Still I dutifully applied the antibacterial foam from the wall-mounted dispenser to my sweaty palms and exchanged pleasantries with the reception staff – one of whom had sought my advice on his creative writing, and how horrific was that?

I had been gripped by the circularity of my fate, which seemed to have been encrypted in the circulation of my blood. What goes around comes around, and this professional needlework was the appropriate karmic comeback for all that amateur embroidery. But as the weeks passed and I discovered the nurse who – for me at least – had magic fingers, and who could perform the venesections efficiently and near-painlessly, so my sense of the singularity of my situation receded as well. 'I have some patients,' my haematologist had said, 'who I've maintained purely on venesections for ten to fifteen years.' And so it finally sank in that 'some' meant by no means 'all'. Singularities, like statistics, belong to the realm of the metaphoric – both exist, fraudulently, in a one-on-one relationship to their own, particular metaphrand. But the only real universals are that we all live – and, of course, we all must die.

In the prefatory remarks to her magisterial essay 'Illness as Metaphor', Susan Sontag notes that we are all dual citizens of the kingdom of the well and the kingdom of the sick – although we all prefer to use only the one passport. She goes on to observe that, of course, illness is not a metaphor at all 'and that the most truthful way of regarding illness – and the healthiest way of being ill – is one most purified of, most resistant to, metaphoric thinking'. I had known this once, yet preoccupied by my own history of mental distress and blinded by my professional malaise – for does not the fiction-maker engorge himself with the similitude of disparate things? – I had looked feverishly for what my bloody disorder was *like*. It seemed synonymous with my addictive illness – and also to be a bizarre antonym of vampirism, which, in turn, surely, was a metaphor for venereal disease? And also for tuberculosis, which in the 1900s was still viewed as repressive of an inflamed and passionate sexual appetite. I had trafficked in illness as metaphor, dealing as a novelist especially in that romanticizing of madness that Sontag sees as 'reflect(ing) in the most vehement way the contemporary prestige of irrational or rude (spontaneous) behaviour (acting out) . . .'

As I got over my culture shock and came to my senses in the realm of the sick I saw that the comfort of things-in-themselves was the only pabulum available or required. The blood pressure cuff cinching my arm, the sensor clipped on to my finger, the nurses in their filmy polythene aprons – to accept these quotidian things was to be open to *every*thing. One of my friends with leukaemia had died – the other was about to have a stem-cell transplant. The friend who'd had his tongue and throat therapeutically mutilated lay in bed twenty hours a day, zonked out by the horror of it all. My wife's cancer had a better than 40 per cent chance of recurring within a decade. Even if statistics weren't for individuals this represented a powerful index of the fact that shit happens. We were middle-aged, apoptosis was well under way – get over it.

Only a culture that had misheard Sontag's advice and instead of excising the cancerously metaphoric assumed that it took benign forms could have witnessed such terrifyingly silly metastases. We may have tried to normalize cancer with fun runs and awareness weeks – yet still we 'battle' against it in a war without end. We may have tried to 'normalize' the condition of the disabled – yet still our only way of doing this is to organize an expensive Paralympics. We don't want ordinary cripples – only elite ones. Death, the real simile for disease – for when we are ill, do we not always feel like we are dying, even if it's only a little? – remains, despite our secularism, the most metaphoricized phenomenon of all, the irony being that so-called assisted suicide hopes to make of quitting this world a simple medical procedure.

As fast as we could eliminate the metaphors – our science helped them to proliferate. Metaphors were the iatrogenic disease of our era. What, I wondered, would Sontag have made of a gastric band or a portosystemic shunt – let alone anal bleaching? As for me, I had always relied on the hardiness of my body to aid me in the battle against my fervid mind – yet now I had cause to examine the last few months it struck me that my sensibility had been doing good therapeutic work well before my diagnosis. The novel I was working on concerned illness – no surprises there. Indeed, it was more than usually saturated with pathology since its protagonist was a sort of disease personified. Yet what was the device I had decided upon in order to lend a verisimilitude to this particularly deranged tale? Why? That there should be no metaphors in it *at all*, nothing should be defined in terms of anything else – no vampire should be like a filthy leech, any more than a filthy leech should be like a vampire. In *Ecce Homo* Nietzsche said that illness was the beginning of all psychology; he might have added that the only possible therapy was a statement of the facts. ■

YOUR BIRTHDAY HAS COME AND GONE

Paul Auster

Your birthday has come and gone. Sixty-four years old now, inching ever closer to senior citizenship, to the days of Medicare and Social Security benefits, to a time when more and more of your friends will have left you. So many of them are gone already – but just wait for the deluge that is coming. Much to your relief, the event passed without incident or commotion, you calmly took it in your stride, a small dinner with friends in Brooklyn, and the impossible age you have now reached seldom entered your thoughts. February third, just one day after your mother's birthday, who went into labour with you on the morning she turned twenty-two, nineteen days before it was supposed to happen, and when the doctor pulled you out of her drugged body with a pair of forceps, it was twenty minutes past midnight, less than half an hour after her birthday had ended. You therefore always celebrated your birthdays together, and even now, almost nine years after her death, you inevitably think about her whenever the clock turns from the second of February to the third. What an unlikely present you must have been that night sixty-four years ago: a baby boy for her birthday, a birth to celebrate her birth.

May 2002. On Saturday, the long, highly spirited conversation with your mother on the telephone, at the end of which you turn to your wife and say: 'She hasn't sounded this happy in years.' On Sunday, your wife leaves for Minnesota. A large celebration for her father's eightieth birthday has been planned for next weekend, and she is going to Northfield in order to help her mother with the arrangements. You stay behind in New York with your daughter, who is fourteen and must attend school, but the two of you will of course be travelling to Minnesota for the party as well, and your tickets have been booked for Friday. In anticipation of the event, you have already written a humorous rhyming poem in your father-in-law's honour – which is the only kind of poem you write any more: frivolous bagatelles for birthdays, weddings, and other family occasions. Monday comes and goes, and everything that happened that day has been obliterated from your memory. On Tuesday, you have a one o'clock meeting with a Frenchwoman in her mid-twenties who has been living in New York for the past several years. She has been engaged by a French publisher to write a guidebook of the city, and because you like this person and feel she is a promising writer, you have agreed to talk to her about New York, doubtful that anything you say will be of much use to her project, but nevertheless you are willing to give it a try. At noon, you are standing in front of the bathroom mirror with shaving cream on your face, about to pick up the razor and begin the job of making yourself presentable for the interview, but before you can attack a single whisker, the telephone rings. You go into the bedroom to answer it, awkwardly positioning the receiver in your hand so as not to cover it with shaving cream, and the voice on the other end is sobbing, the person who has called you is in a state of extreme distress, and little by little you understand that it is Debbie, the young woman who cleans your mother's apartment once a week and occasionally drives her on errands, and what Debbie is telling you now is that she just let herself into the apartment and found your mother on the bed, your mother's body on the bed, your dead mother's body on the bed. Your insides seem to empty out as you take in the news. You feel dazed and hollow, unable to think, and even if this is the last thing you were expecting to happen now (*She hasn't sounded this happy in years*), you are not surprised by what Debbie is telling you, not stunned, not shocked, not even upset. What is wrong with you? you ask yourself. Your mother has just died, and you've turned into a block of wood. You tell Debbie to wait where she is, you will get there as quickly as you can (Verona, New Jersey – next to Montclair), and an hour and a half later you are in your mother's apartment, looking at her corpse on the bed. You have seen several corpses in the past, and you are familiar with the inertness of the dead, the inhuman stillness that envelops the bodies of the no longer living, but none of those corpses belonged to your mother, no other dead body was the body in which your own life began, and you can look for no more than a few seconds before you turn your head away. The blue-tinged pallor of her skin, her half-closed eyes fixed on nothing, an extinguished self lying on top of the covers in her nightgown and bathrobe, the Sunday paper sprawled around her, one bare leg dangling over the edge of the bed, a spot of white drool hardened in a corner of her mouth. You cannot look at her, you will not look at her, you find it unbearable to look at her, and yet even after the paramedics have wheeled her out of the apartment in a black body bag, you continue to feel nothing. No tears, no howls of anguish, no grief – just a vague sense of horror growing inside you. Your cousin Regina is with you now, your mother's first cousin, who has driven over from her house in nearby Glen Ridge to lend you a hand, the daughter of your grandfather's only brother, five or six years younger than your mother, your first cousin once removed and one of the few people on either side of your family you feel any connection to, an artist, widow of another artist, the young bohemian woman who fled Brooklyn in the early fifties to live in the Village, and she stays with you throughout the day, she and her grown daughter Anna, the two of them helping you sort through your mother's belongings and papers, conferring with you as you struggle to decide what to do about someone who left no will and never talked about her wishes after death (burial or cremation, funeral or no funeral), making lists with you of all the practical tasks that must be dealt with sooner rather than later, and that evening, after dinner in a restaurant, they take you back to their house and show you the guest room where you can spend the night. Your daughter is staying with friends in Park Slope, your wife is with her parents in Minnesota, and after a long talk with her on the phone after dinner, you are unable to sleep. You have bought a bottle of Scotch to keep you company, and so you sit in a downstairs room until three or four in the morning, consuming half the bottle of Oban as you try to think about your mother, but your mind is still too numb to think about much of anything. Scattered thoughts, inconsequential thoughts, and still no impulse to cry, to break down and mourn your mother with an earnest display of sorrow and regret. Perhaps you are afraid of what will happen to you if you let yourself go, that once you allow yourself to cry you will not be able to stop yourself, that the pain will be too crushing and you will fall to pieces, and because you don't want to risk losing control of yourself, you hold on to the pain, swallow it, bury it in your heart. You miss your wife, miss her more than at any time since you have been married, for she is the only person who knows you well enough to ask the right questions, who has the assurance and understanding to prod you into revealing things about yourself that often elude your own understanding, and how much better it would be if you were lying in bed with her now instead of sitting alone in a darkened room at three in the morning with a bottle of whisky. The next morning, your cousins continue to prop you up and help you with the tasks at hand, the visit to the mortuary and the selection of an urn (after consulting with your wife, your mother's sister, and your cousin, the unanimous decision was cremation and no funeral, with a memorial service to be held sometime after the summer), the calls to the real estate man, the car man, the furniture man, the cable television man, all the men you must contact in order to sell, disconnect, and discard, and then, after a long day submerged in the bleak miasma of *nothing*, they drive you back to your house in Brooklyn. You all share a takeout dinner with your daughter, you thank Regina for having *saved your life* (your exact words, since you truly don't know what you would have done without her), and once they have left, you stay up for a while talking to your daughter, but eventually she marches upstairs to go to bed, and now that you are alone again, you again find yourself resisting the lure of sleep. The second night is a repetition of the first: sitting alone in a darkened room with the same bottle of Scotch, which you drain to the bottom this time, and still no tears, no cogent thoughts, and no inclination to call it a night and turn in. After many hours, exhaustion finally overwhelms you, and when you fall into bed at five thirty, dawn is already breaking outside and the birds have begun to sing. You plan to sleep for as long as possible, ten or twelve hours if you can manage it, knowing that oblivion is the only cure for you now, but just after eight o'clock, when you have been sleeping for roughly two and a half hours, and sleeping in a way that only the drunk can sleep – *profondamente, stupidamente* – the telephone rings. If the phone were on the other side of the room, it is doubtful you would even hear it, but there it is on the nightstand next to your pillow, not twelve inches from your head, eleven inches from your right ear, and after how many rings (you will never know how many), your eyes involuntarily open. During those first seconds of semi-consciousness, you understand that you have never felt worse, that your body is no longer the body you are used to calling your own, that this new and alien physical self has been hammered by a hundred wooden mallets, dragged by horses for a hundred miles over a barren terrain of rocks and cacti, reduced to a heap of dust by a hundred-ton pile driver. Your bloodstream is so saturated with alcohol that you can smell it coming out of your pores, and the entire room stinks of bad breath and whisky – fetid, noxious, disgusting. If you want anything now, if one wish could be granted to you, even at the cost of giving up ten years of your life in exchange, it is simply to shut your eyes again and go back to sleep. And yet, for reasons you will never understand (force of habit? a sense of duty? a conviction that the caller is your wife?), you roll over, extend your arm, and pick up the phone. It is one of your cousins, a female first cousin from your father's side of the family, ten years older than you are and a contentious, self-appointed moral judge, the last person on earth you want to talk to, but now that you have picked up the phone, you can't very well hang up on her, not when she is talking, talking, talking, scarcely pausing long enough to let you say a word, to give you a chance to break in and cut the conversation short. How is it possible, you wonder, for someone to rattle on as quickly as she does? It is as if she has trained herself not to breathe while she talks, to spew forth entire paragraphs in a single, uninterrupted exhale, long outrushes of verbiage with no punctuation and no need to stop for an occasional intake of air. Her lungs must be enormous, you think, the largest lungs in the world, and such stamina, such a burning compulsion to have the last word on every subject. You and this cousin have had numerous battles in the past, beginning with the publication of *The Invention of Solitude* in 1982, which in her eyes constituted a betrayal of Auster family secrets (your grandmother murdered your grandfather in 1919), and henceforth you were turned into an outcast, just as your mother was turned into an outcast after she and your father divorced (which is why you have decided against a funeral for her – in order to avoid having to invite certain members of that clan to the service), but at the same time this cousin is not a stupid woman, she is a summa cum laude college graduate, a psychologist with a large and successful practice, an expansive, energetic person who always makes a point of telling you how many of her friends read your novels, and it is true that she has made some efforts to patch things up between you over the years, to nullify the damage of her vicious outburst against your book two decades ago, but even if she professes to admire you now, there is nevertheless an abiding rancour in her as well, an animosity that continues to lurk inside her overtures of friendship, none of it is purely one thing or the other, and the whole situation between you is fraught with complications, for her health is not good, she has been undergoing cancer treatments for some time and you can't help feeling sorry for her, and because she has taken the trouble to call, you want to give her the benefit of the doubt, to allow her this short, perfunctory conversation and then roll over and go back to sleep. She begins by saying all the appropriate things. How sudden, how unexpected, how unprepared you must have been, and think of your sister, your poor schizophrenic sister, how will she cope now that your mother is gone? That is enough, you feel, more than enough to demonstrate her goodwill and sympathy, and you hope you will be able to hang up after another sentence or two, since your eyes are closing now, you are absolutely miserable with exhaustion, and if she would only stop talking within the next few seconds, you would have no trouble drifting off again into the deepest of slumbers. But your cousin is just getting started, rolling up her sleeves and spitting into her hands, as it were, and for the next five minutes she shares her earliest memories of your mother with you, meeting her as a girl of nine when your mother was still so young herself, just twenty or twenty-one, and how thrilling it was to have such a pretty new aunt in the family, so warm and full of life, and so you go on listening, you don't have the strength to interrupt her, and before long she is on another subject altogether, you don't know how she got there, but suddenly you hear her voice talking to you about your smoking, imploring you to stop, to give it up for good, or else you will become sick and die, die a horrendous early death, and as you die you will be filled with remorse for having *murdered yourself* in such a thoughtless way. She has been at it for nine or ten minutes at this point, and you are beginning to worry that you will not be able to go back to sleep, for the longer she goes on, the more you feel yourself being pulled toward consciousness, and once the line is crossed, there will be no turning back. You can't survive on two and a half hours' sleep, not in your present condition, not with so much alcohol still in your blood, you will be destroyed for the whole day, but even though you are feeling more and more tempted to hang up on her, you cannot find the will to do it. Then comes the onslaught, the barrage of verbal cannon fire you should have been expecting from the instant you picked up the phone. How could you have been so naive as to think that kind words and quasi-hysterical warnings would be the end of it? There is still the question of your mother's character to be dealt with, and even if her body was discovered only two days ago, even if the crematorium in New Jersey has scheduled her body to be burned into ashes this very afternoon, that doesn't prevent your cousin from letting her have it. Thirty-eight years after she left your father, the family has codified its litany of complaints against your mother, it is the stuff of ancestral history by now, old gossip turned into solid facts, and why not go through the list of her misdeeds one last time – in order to give her a proper send-off to the place where she deserves to go? Never satisfied, your cousin says, always looking for something else, too flirtatious for her own good, a woman who lived and breathed to attract the attentions of men, oversexed, whorish, someone who slept around, an unfaithful wife – too bad that a person with so many other good qualities should have been such a mess. You always suspected your mother's ex-in-laws talked about her in that way, but until this morning you have never heard it with your own ears. You mumble something into the telephone and hang up, vowing never to talk to your cousin again, never to utter a single word to her for the rest of your life. Sleep is out of the question now. In spite of the supernatural exhaustion that has clobbered you into near senselessness, too much has been churned up inside you, your thoughts are sprinting off in myriad directions, adrenalin is surging through your system again, and your eyes refuse to close. There is nothing for it but to get out of bed and begin the day. You go downstairs and prepare a pot of coffee, the strongest, blackest coffee you have made in years, figuring that if you flood yourself with titanic doses of caffeine, you will be lifted into something that resembles wakefulness, a partial wakefulness, which will allow you to sleepwalk through the rest of the morning and on into the afternoon. You drink the first cup slowly. It is exceedingly hot and must be swallowed in small sips, but then the coffee begins to cool down, and you drink the second cup more rapidly than the first, the third more rapidly than the second, and swallow by swallow the liquid splashes into your empty stomach like acid. You can feel the caffeine accelerating your heart rate, agitating your nerves and beginning to light you up. You are awake now, fully awake and yet still weary, drained but ever more alert, and in your head there is a buzzing that wasn't there before, a low-pitched mechanical sound, a humming, a whining, as if from a distant, out-of-tune radio, and the more you drink, the more you feel your body changing, the less you feel that you are made of flesh and blood. You are turning into something metallic now, a rusty contraption that simulates human life, a thing put together with wires and fuses, vast circuits of wires controlled by random electrical impulses, and now that you have finished the third cup of coffee, you pour yourself another – which turns out to be the last one, the lethal one. The attack begins simultaneously from the inside and the outside, a sudden feeling of pressure from the air around you, as if an invisible force were trying to push you through the chair and knock you to the ground, but at the same time an unearthly lightness in your head, a vertiginous jangle thrumming against the walls of your skull, and all the while the outside continues to press in on you, even as the inside grows empty, ever more dark and empty, as if you are about to pass out. Then your pulse quickens, you can feel your heart trying to burst through your chest, and a moment after that there is no more air in your lungs, you can no longer breathe. That is when the panic overwhelms you, when your body shuts down and you fall to the floor. Lying on your back, you feel the blood stop flowing in your veins, and little by little your limbs turn to cement. That is when you start to howl. You are made of stone now, and as you lie there on the dining-room floor, rigid, your mouth open, unable to move or think, you howl in terror as you wait for your body to drown in the deep black waters of death.

You couldn't cry. You couldn't grieve in the way people normally do, and so your body broke down and did the grieving for you. If not for the various incidental factors that preceded the onset of panic (your wife's absence, the alcohol, the lack of sleep, your cousin's phone call, the coffee), it is possible the attack never would have taken place. But in the end those elements are of only secondary importance. The question is why you couldn't let yourself go in the minutes and hours that followed your mother's death, why, for two full days, you were unable to shed any tears for her. Was it because a part of you was secretly glad she was dead? A dark thought, a thought so dark and disturbing that it scares you even to express it, but even if you are willing to entertain the possibility that it is true, you doubt that it would account for your failure to cry. You didn't cry after your father's death either. Nor after the deaths of your grandparents, nor after the death of your most beloved cousin, who died of breast cancer when she was thirty-eight, nor after the deaths of the many friends who have left you over the years. Not even at fourteen, when you were less than a foot away from a boy who was struck and killed by lightning, the boy whose dead body you sat next to and watched over for the next hour in a rain-drenched meadow, desperately trying to warm up his body and revive him because you didn't understand he was dead – not even that monstrous death could coax a single tear from you. Your eyes water up when you watch certain movies, you have dropped tears onto the pages of numerous books, you have cried at moments of immense personal sorrow, but death freezes you and shuts you down, robbing you of all emotion, all affect, all connection to your own heart. From the very beginning, you have gone dead in the face of death, and that is what happened to you with your mother's death as well. At least for the first little while, the first two days and nights, but then lightning struck again, and you were scorched.

Forget what your cousin said to you on the phone. You were angry at her, yes, appalled that she would stoop to slinging mud at such an inappropriate time, revolted by her nastiness, her sanctimonious contempt for a person who never did her an ounce of harm, but her accusations of infidelity against your mother were old business to you by then, and even if you had no proof, no evidence to support or deny the charges, you had long suspected that your mother *might* have strayed during her marriage to your father. You were fifty-five years old when you had that conversation with your cousin, and with so much time to have pondered the details of your parents' unfortunate marriage, you in fact hoped that your mother had found some comfort with another man (or men). But nothing was certain, and only once did you have any inkling that something might be amiss, a single moment when you were twelve or thirteen, which thoroughly perplexed you at the time: walking into the house one day after school, thinking no one else was there, picking up the telephone to make a call, and hearing a man's voice on the line, a voice that did not belong to your father, saying no more than *Goodbye,* an altogether neutral word perhaps, but spoken with great tenderness, and then your mother saying back to him, *Goodbye, darling.* That was the end of the conversation. You had no idea what the context was, could not identify the man, had heard almost nothing, and yet you worried about it for days, so much so that you finally found the courage to ask your mother about it, she who had always been honest and direct with you, you felt, who had never refused to answer your questions, but this time, this one time, she looked puzzled when you told her what you had heard, as if she had been caught off guard, and then a moment later she laughed, saying she couldn't remember, she didn't know what you were talking about. It was entirely possible that she didn't remember, that the conversation was of no importance and the endearment had not meant what you thought it had, but a tiny germ of doubt was planted in your head that day, doubt that quickly vanished in the weeks and months that followed, but four or five years later, when your mother announced that she was leaving your father, you couldn't help thinking back to the last sentences of that accidentally overheard conversation. Did any of it matter? No, not that you could think of. Your parents had been destined to split up from the day they were married, and whether your mother had slept with the man she called *darling,* whether there was another man or several men or no man at all, did not play a part in their divorce. Symptoms are not causes, and whatever ugly little thoughts your cousin might have harboured against your mother, she knew nothing about anything. It is undeniable that her call helped to unleash your panic attack – the timing of the call, the circumstances of the call – but what she said to you that morning was stale news.

O n the other hand, even though you happened to be her son, you know next to nothing yourself. Too many gaps, too many silences and evasions, too many threads lost over the years for you to stitch together a coherent story. Useless to talk about her from the outside, then. Whatever can be told must be pulled from the inside, from your insides, the accumulation of memories and perceptions you continue to carry around in your body – and which left you, for reasons that will never be entirely known, gasping for breath on the dining-room floor, certain you were about to die.

A hasty, ill-considered marriage, an impetuous marriage between two incompatible souls that ran out of steam before the honeymoon was over. A twenty-one-year-old girl from New York (born and bred in Brooklyn, translated to Manhattan at sixteen) and a thirty-four-year-old bachelor from Newark who had begun life in Wisconsin and had left there, fatherless, at the age of seven, when your grandmother shot and killed your grandfather in the kitchen of their house. The bride was the younger of two daughters, the product of yet another ill-considered, mismatched marriage (*Your father would be such a wonderful man – if only he were different*) who had dropped out of high school to work (clerical jobs in offices, later a photographer's assistant) and never told you much about her earlier loves and romances. A vague story about a boyfriend who had died in the war, an even vaguer story about a brief flirtation with actor Steve Cochran, but beyond that nothing at all. She finished up her diploma by going to school at night (Commercial High), but no college afterward, and no college for your father either, who was still a boy when he entered the Land of Work and began supporting himself as soon as he graduated from high school at eighteen. Those are the known facts, the few bits of verifiable information that have been passed down to you. Then come the invisible years, the first three or four years of your life, the blank time before any possibility of recall, and therefore you have nothing to go on but the various stories your mother told you later: your near death at sixteen months from tonsillitis (106-degree fever, and the doctor telling her: *It's in God's hands now*), the vagaries of your cranky, disobedient stomach, a condition that was diagnosed as an allergy or intolerance to something (wheat? gluten?) and forced you to subsist for two and a half years on a diet limited almost exclusively to bananas (so many bananas consumed in that time before memory that you still recoil from the sight and smell of them and have not eaten one in sixty years), the jutting nail that tore apart your cheek in the Newark department store in 1950, your remarkable ability at age three to identify the make and model of every car on the road (remarkable to your mother, who read it as a sign of incipient genius), but most of all the pleasure she communicated to you in the telling of these stories, the way she seemed to exult in the mere fact of your existence, and because her marriage was such an unhappy one, you realize now that she turned to you as a form of consolation, to give her life a meaning and a purpose it was otherwise lacking. You were the beneficiary of her unhappiness, and you were well loved, especially well loved, without question deeply loved. That first of all, that above and beyond everything else there might be to say: she was an ardent and dedicated mother to you during your infancy and early childhood, and whatever is good in you now, whatever strengths you might possess, come from that time before you can remember who you were.

Some early glimmers, a few small islands of recollection in an otherwise endless sea of black. Waiting for your newborn sister to come home from the hospital with your parents (age: three years and nine months), looking through the slats of the venetian blinds in the living room with your mother's mother and leaping up and down when the car finally stopped in front of the house. According to your mother, you were an enthusiastic older brother, not at all envious of the new baby who had entered your midst, but she seems to have handled the matter with great intelligence, not shutting you out but turning you into her *helper*, which gave you the illusion that you were actively participating in your sister's care. Some months later, you were asked if you wanted to give nursery school a try. You said yes, not quite sure what nursery school was, since preschools were far

less common in 1951 than they are now, but after one day you had
had enough. You remember having to line up with a group of other
children and pretend you were in a grocery store, and when your
turn finally came, after what seemed to have been hours, you handed
a pile of pretend money to someone standing behind a pretend cash
register, who gave you a bag of pretend food in return. You told
your mother that nursery school was an idiotic waste of time, and
she didn't try to talk you into going back. Then your family moved
to the house on Irving Avenue, and when you started kindergarten
the following September, you were ready for school, not the least
bit fazed by the prospect of spending time away from your mother.
You remember the chaotic prelude to the first morning, the children
who ranted and screamed when their mothers said goodbye to them,
the anguished cries of the abandoned echoing off the walls as you
calmly waved goodbye to your own mother, and all that fuss was
incomprehensible to you, since you were happy to be there and felt
like a big person now. You were five years old, and already you were
pulling away, no longer living exclusively in your mother's orbit.
Better health, new friends, the freedom of the yard behind the house,
and the beginnings of an autonomous life. You still wet the bed, of
course, you still cried when you fell down and cut your knee, but the
inner dialogue had begun, and you had crossed into the domain of
conscious selfhood. Nevertheless, because of the hours he put in at
work, and because of his penchant for taking long naps whenever
he was at home, your father was largely absent from the household,
and your mother continued to be the central force of authority and
wisdom for all things that counted most. She was the one who put
you to bed, the one who taught you how to ride a bicycle, the one who
helped you with your piano lessons, the one you unburdened yourself
to, the rock you clung to whenever the seas grew rough. But you were
developing a mind of your own, and you were no longer in thrall
to her every pronouncement and opinion. You hated practising the
piano, you wanted to be outside playing with your friends, and when
you told her that you would prefer to quit, that baseball was vastly

more important to you than music, she relented without putting up much of an argument. Then there was the issue of clothes. You mostly ran around in a T-shirt and a pair of jeans (called dungarees back then), but for special occasions – holidays, birthday parties, the visits to your grandparents in New York – she insisted on dressing you in finely tailored outfits, clothes that began to embarrass you by the time you reached six, especially the white-shirt-and-short-pants combo with the knee socks and sandals, and when you began to protest, claiming that you felt ridiculous in those things, that all you wanted was to look like every other American boy, she eventually gave ground and allowed you to have a say in what you wore. But she was pulling away by then, too, and not long after you turned six, she went off to the Land of Work, and you began seeing less and less of her. You don't remember feeling sad about it, but then again, what do you really know about what you felt? The important thing to keep in mind is that you know next to nothing – and nothing whatsoever about the state of her marriage, the depth of her unhappiness with your father. Years later, she told you that she tried to talk him into moving to California, that she felt there would be no hope for them unless he got away from his family, the suffocating presence of his mother and older brothers, and when he refused to consider it, she resigned herself to a marriage of no hope. The children were too small for her to contemplate divorce (not then, not there, not in middle-class America of the early fifties), and so she found another solution. She was only twenty-eight years old, and work opened the door, let her out of the house, and gave her a chance to build a life of her own.

You don't mean to suggest that she disappeared. She was simply less present than before, far less present, and if most of your memories from that period are confined to the little world of your boyhood pursuits (running around with your friends, riding your bicycle, going to school, playing sports, collecting stamps and baseball cards, reading comic books), your mother appears vividly in several instances, particularly when you were eight and for some reason joined the Cub Scouts with a dozen or so of your friends. You can't remember how often the meetings were held, but you suspect it was once a month, each time in the house of a different member, and these gatherings were run by a rotating squad of three or four women, the so-called den mothers, one of whom was your own mother, which proves that her work as a real estate broker was not so crushing that she couldn't afford to take an occasional afternoon off. You remember how much you enjoyed seeing her in her navy-blue den mother's uniform (the absurdity of it, the novelty of it), and you also remember that she was the den mother the boys liked best, for she was the youngest and prettiest of all the mothers, the most entertaining, the most relaxed, the one who had no trouble commanding their complete attention. You can recall two of the meetings she ran with utmost clarity: working on the construction of wooden storage boxes (for what purpose you can no longer say, but everyone applied himself to the task with great diligence), and then, toward the end of the school year, when the weather was warm and the entire gang had grown bored with the rules and regulations of Scouthood, there was a last or next-to-last meeting at your house on Irving Avenue, and because no one had the stomach for pretending to act like miniature soldiers any more, your mother asked the boys how they would like to spend the afternoon, and when the unanimous response was *play baseball*, you all went out into the backyard and picked up sides for a game. Because there were only ten or twelve of you and the teams were shorthanded, your mother decided to play as well. You were immensely pleased, but since you had never seen her swing a bat, you weren't expecting her to do much of anything but strike out. When she came up in the second inning and smacked a ball far over the left fielder's head, you were more than pleased, you were flabbergasted. You can still see your mother running around the bases in her den mother's uniform and coming in to the plate with her home run – out of breath, smiling, soaking up the cheers from the boys. Of all the memories you have retained of her from your childhood, this is the one that comes back to you most often.

She probably wasn't beautiful, not beautiful in the classic sense of the term, but pretty enough, more than attractive enough to make men stare at her whenever she walked into a room. What she lacked in the way of pure good looks, the movie-star looks of certain women who may or may not be movie stars, she made up for by exuding an aura of glamour, especially when she was young, from her late twenties to her early forties, a mysterious combination of carriage, poise and elegance, the clothes that pointed to but did not overstate the sensuality of the person inside them, the perfume, the make-up, the jewellery, the stylishly coiffed hair, and, above all, the playful look in the eyes, at once forthright and demure, *a look of confidence*, and even if she wasn't the most beautiful woman in the world, she acted as if she were, and a woman who can pull that off will inevitably make heads turn, which was no doubt what caused the dour matrons of your father's family to despise her after she left the fold. Those were difficult years, of course, the stretch of years before the long-deferred but inevitable break-up with your father, the years of *Goodbye, darling* and the car she wrecked one night when you were ten. You can still see her bloodied, banged-up face as she walked into the house early the next morning, and although she never told you much about the accident, only a bland, generic account that must have had little to do with the truth, you suspect that alcohol might have been involved, that there was a short period back then when she was drinking too much, for later on she dropped some hints about having been in AA, and the fact was that she never drank any alcohol for the rest of her life – not one cocktail or glass of champagne, nothing, not even a sip of beer.

There were three of her, three separate women who seemed unconnected to one another, and as you grew older and began to look at her differently, to see her as someone who was not just your mother, you never knew which mask she would be wearing on any given day. At one end, there was the diva, the sumptuously decked-out charmer who dazzled the world in public, the young woman with the obtuse, distracted husband who craved having the eyes of others upon her and would not allow herself – not any more – to be boxed into the role of traditional housewife. In the middle, which was far and away the largest space she occupied, there was a solid and responsible being, a person of intelligence and compassion, the woman who took care of you when you were young, the woman who went out to work, who ran several small businesses over the course of many years, the four-star joke teller and crossword-puzzle ace, a person with her feet firmly planted on the ground – competent, generous, observant of the world around her, a devoted liberal in her politics, a sage dispenser of advice. At the other end, the extreme end of who she was, there was the frightened and debilitated neurotic, the helpless creature prey to blistering assaults of anxiety, the phobic whose incapacities grew as the years advanced – from an early fear of heights to a metastatic flowering of multiple forms of paralysis: afraid of escalators, afraid of airplanes, afraid of elevators, afraid to drive a car, afraid of going near windows on the upper floors of buildings, afraid to be alone, afraid of open spaces, afraid to walk anywhere (she felt she would lose her balance or pass out), and an ever-present hypochondria that gradually reached the most exalted summits of dread. In other words: afraid to die, which in the end is probably no different from saying: afraid to live. When you were young, you were not aware of any of this. She seemed perfect to you, and even during her first attack of vertigo, which you happened to witness when you were six (the two of you climbing up the inner staircase of the Statue of Liberty), you were not alarmed, because she was a good and conscientious mother, and she managed to hide her fear from you by turning the descent into a game: sitting on the stairs together and going down one step at a time, asses on the rungs, laughing all the way to the bottom. When she was old, there was no more laughter. Only the void spinning around in her head, the knot in her belly, the cold sweats, a pair of invisible hands tightening around her throat.

Her second marriage was a grand success, the marriage everyone longs for – until it wasn't. You were glad to see her so happy, so clearly in love, and you took to her new husband without hesitation, not only because he was in love with your mother and knew how to love her in all the ways you felt she needed to be loved, but because he was an impressive man in his own right, a labour lawyer with an acute mind and a large personality, someone who seemed to take life by storm, who boomed out old standards at the dinner table and told hilarious stories about his past, who instantly embraced you not as a stepson but as a kind of younger brother, which turned you into close, steadfast friends, and all in all you thought this marriage was the best thing that had ever happened to your mother, the thing that would make everything right for her at last. She was still young, after all, still not forty years old, and because he was two years younger than she was, you had every reason to expect they would have a long life together and die in each other's arms. But your stepfather's health was not good. Strong and vigorous as he seemed, he had been cursed with a bad heart, and after a first coronary in his early thirties, he had his second big attack about a year into the marriage, and from then on there was an element of foreboding that hung over their life together, which only worsened when he suffered a third attack a couple of years later. Your mother lived in constant fear of losing him, and you saw with your own eyes how those fears gradually unhinged her, little by little exacerbating the weaknesses she had struggled for so long to keep hidden, the phobic self that roared into full bloom during their last years together, and when he died at fifty-four, she was no longer the person she had been when they were married. You remember her last heroic stand, the night in Palo Alto, California, when she told jokes non-stop to you and your wife as your stepfather lay in the intensive care unit of the Stanford Medical Center undergoing experimental cardiac treatments. The final, desperate move in a case that had been deemed all but hopeless, and the gruesome sight of your mortally ill stepfather lying in that bed hooked up to so many wires and machines that the room looked like the set from a science-fiction film, and when you walked in and saw him there, you were so stunned and miserable that you found yourself fighting back tears. It was the summer of 1981, and you and your wife had known each other for about six months, you were living together but not yet married, and as the two of you stood at your stepfather's bedside, he reached out, took hold of both your hands, and said: 'Don't waste any time. Get married now. Get married, take care of each other, and have twelve children.' You and your wife were staying with your mother in a house somewhere in Palo Alto, an empty house that had been lent to her by some unknown friend, and that night, after eating dinner in a restaurant, where you nearly broke down again when the waitress came back to tell you that the kitchen had run out of the dish you had ordered (displaced anguish in its most pronounced form – to such a degree that the nonsensical tears you felt gathering in your eyes might be interpreted as the very embodiment of repressed emotions that can no longer be repressed), and once the three of you had returned to the house, the gloom of a house shadowed in death, all of you convinced that these were the last days of your stepfather's life, you sat down at the dining-room table to have a drink, and just when you thought it would be impossible for anyone to say another word, when the heaviness in your hearts seemed to have crushed all the words out of you, your mother started telling jokes. One joke and then another joke, then another joke followed by the next joke, jokes so funny that you and your wife laughed until you could hardly breathe any more, an hour of jokes, two hours of jokes, each one delivered with such crackerjack timing, such crisp, economical language that a moment came when you thought your stomach might burst through your skin. Jewish jokes mostly, an unending torrent of classic yenta routines with all the appropriate voices and accents, the old Jewish women sitting around a card table and sighing, each one sighing in turn, each one sighing more loudly that the last, until one of the women finally says, 'I thought we agreed not to talk about the children.' You all went a little crazy that night, but the circumstances were so grim and intolerable that you needed to go a little crazy, and somehow your mother managed to find the strength to let that happen. A moment of extraordinary courage, you felt, a sublime instance of who she was at her best – for great as your misery was that night, you knew that it was nothing, absolutely nothing compared to hers.

He survived the Stanford Medical Center and went home, but less than a year later he was dead. You believe that was when she died as well. Her heart went on beating for another twenty years, but the death of your stepfather was the end of her, and she never regained her footing after that. Little by little, her grief was transformed into a kind of resentment (*How dare he die on me and leave me alone?*) and while it pained you to hear her talk like that, you understood that she was frightened, searching for a way to hazard the next step and hobble on toward the future. She hated living on her own, was temperamentally not equipped to survive in a vacuum of solitude, and before long she was back in circulation, quite heavy now, many pounds overweight, but still attractive enough to turn the heads of several ageing men. She had been living in southern California for over a decade at that point, and you saw each other infrequently, no more than once every six months or so, and what you knew about her was learned mostly through telephone conversations – useful in their way, but you seldom had a chance to observe her in action, and consequently you were both surprised and not surprised when she told you she was planning to get married again after just eighteen months of widowhood. It was a foolish marriage in your opinion, another hasty, ill-considered marriage, not unlike the marriage she made with your father in 1946, but she wasn't looking for a big love any more so much as a refuge, someone to take care of her as she mended her fragile self. In his quiet, fumbling way, the third husband was devoted to her, which certainly counts for something, but for all his efforts and good intentions, he couldn't take care of her well enough. He was a dull man, an ex-marine and former NASA engineer, conservative in both his politics and his manner, either meek or weak (perhaps both), and therefore a one-hundred-

and-eighty-degree turn from your effusive, charismatic, left-liberal stepfather – not a bad or cruel person, simply dull. He now worked as a self-employed inventor (of the struggling variety), but your mother had high hopes for his most recent invention – an intravenous medical device, both tubeless and portable, that would compete with and potentially supplant the traditional IV – and because it looked like a sure thing, she married him on the assumption that they would soon be rolling in money. There is no doubt that it was a clever invention, perhaps even a brilliant one, but the inventor had no head for business. Squeezed between fast-talking venture capitalists and double-talking medical supply firms, he eventually lost control of his own device, and while he walked off with some money in the end, it was hardly enough to roll in – so little, in fact, that within a year most of it was gone. Your mother, who was into her sixties by then, was forced to go back to work. She restarted the interior design business she had shut down some years earlier, and with her inventor husband serving as her office assistant and bookkeeper, she was the one who was supporting them now, or trying to support them, and whenever their bank account was in danger of dipping toward zero, she would call you to ask for help, always tearful, always apologetic, and because you were in a position to give that help, you sent them cheques every so often, some large cheques, some small cheques, about a dozen cheques and wire transfers over the next couple of years. You didn't mind sending them the money, but you found it strange, and more than a little disheartening, that her ex-marine had given up on himself so thoroughly that he was no longer able to pull his weight, that the man who was going to provide for her and lead them into the bower of a comfortable old age could not even summon the courage to thank you for your help. Your mother was the boss now, and bit by bit his role as husband was turned into that of faithful butler (breakfast in bed, shopping for groceries), but still they forged on, it wasn't so bad, surely it could have been worse, and even if she was disappointed by the way things had turned out, she also knew that something was better than nothing. Then, one morning in the spring of 1994, just after she had woken up, your mother walked into the bathroom and found her husband lying dead on the floor. Stroke, heart attack, cerebral haemorrhage – it is impossible to say, since no autopsy was ever performed, at least none that you are aware of. When she called your house in Brooklyn later that morning, her voice was filled with horror. Blood, she said to you, blood coming out of his mouth, blood everywhere, and for the first time in all the years you had known her, she sounded deranged.

She decided to move back east. Twenty years earlier, she had thought of California as a promised land, but now it was little more than a place of disease and death, the capital of bad luck and painful memories, and so she bolted across America to be near her family – you and your wife to begin with, but also her mentally ill daughter in Connecticut, her sister, and her two grandchildren. She was flat broke, of course, which meant that you would have to support her, but that was hardly a problem now, and you were more than willing to do it. You bought her a one-bedroom apartment in Verona, leased a car for her, and gave her what you both considered to be an adequate monthly allowance. You were hardly the first son in the world to find himself in this position, but that didn't make it any less strange or uncomfortable: to be taking care of the person who had once taken care of you, to have reached that point in life when your roles were reversed, with you now acting the part of parent while she was reduced to the part of helpless child. The financial arrangement occasionally caused some friction, since your mother found it difficult not to overspend her allowance, and even though you increased the amount several times, it was still difficult for her, which put you in the awkward spot of having to scold her every now and then, and once, when you were probably a bit too harsh with her, she broke down and cried on the telephone, telling you she was a useless old woman and maybe she should kill herself so she wouldn't be such a burden any more. There was something comical about this gush of self-pity (you knew you were being manipulated), but at the same time it made you feel wretched, and in the end you always caved in and let her have whatever she wanted. More worrisome to you was her inability to do anything, to get out of her apartment and engage herself with the world. You suggested that she volunteer as a reading teacher for struggling children or illiterate adults, get involved with the Democratic Party or some other political organization, take courses, travel, join a social club, but she simply didn't have it in her to try. Until then, the lack of a formal education had never been an impediment to her – her native intelligence and quickness had seemed to make up for any deficiencies – but now that she was without a husband, without work, without anything to keep her occupied from day to day, you wished she could have developed an interest in music or art or books, in anything really, just so long as it was some kind of passionate, sustaining interest, but she had never formed the habit of nurturing inner pursuits of that kind, and therefore she continued to flail around without purpose, never quite sure what to do with herself when she woke up in the morning. The only novels she read were detective stories and thrillers, and even your books and your wife's books, which you both automatically gave her whenever they were published – and which she proudly displayed on a special shelf in her living room – were not the sorts of books she could read. She watched a lot of television. The TV was always on in her apartment, blasting forth from early in the morning until late at night, but it wasn't for watching programmes so much as for the voices that came from the box. Those voices comforted her, were in fact necessary to her, and they helped her overcome her fear of living alone – which was probably her single greatest accomplishment of those years. No, they were not the best years, but you don't want to give the impression that it was a time of unbroken melancholy and disarray. She made regular visits to Connecticut to see your sister, spent countless weekends with you at your house in Brooklyn, saw her granddaughter perform in school plays and sing her solos for the school chorus, followed her grandson's ever-deepening interest in photography, and after all those years in distant California, she was now a part of your life again, always present for birthdays, holidays, and special events – public appearances by you and your wife, the openings of your films (she was mad for the movies), and occasional dinners with your friends. She continued to charm people in public, even into her mid-seventies, for in some small corner of her mind she still saw herself as a star, as the most beautiful woman in the world, and whenever she emerged from her diminished, largely shut-in life, her vanity seemed to be intact. So much of what she had become saddened you now, but you found it impossible not to admire her for that vanity, for still being able to tell a good joke when people were listening.

You scattered her ashes in the woods of Prospect Park. There were five of you present that day – your wife, your daughter, your aunt, your cousin Regina, and yourself – and you chose Prospect Park in Brooklyn because your mother had played there often as a little girl. One by one, you all read poems out loud, and then, as you opened the rectangular metal urn and tossed the ashes on to the fallen leaves and underbrush, your aunt (normally undemonstrative, one of the most reserved people you have ever known) gave in to a fit of tears as she repeated the name of her baby sister over and over again. A week or two later, on a sparkling afternoon in late May, you and your wife took your dog for a walk in the park. You suggested returning to the spot where you had scattered your mother's ashes, but when you were still out on an open path, a good two hundred yards from the edge of the woods, you started feeling faint and dizzy, and even though you were taking pills to keep your new condition under control, you could feel another panic attack coming on. You took hold of your wife's arm, and the two of you turned around and went home. That was nearly nine years ago. You have not tried to go back to those woods since. ∎

Quarantine

Sounds like a miner's melody. Or a gemstone set in platinum.
A set of blonde and imbricated petals. The perplexing swish
of botany's haste. A season originates, then gratifies and ends.
Sounds like so many things that happen as *beyond*.

Now entering. Solve all arboreal problems that you can.
Then what to do when boxelder bugs aren't rampant:
that's a different set of worries. Play worry in different keys.
C is where you always start and end. Or so my teacher said.

For he was taken by the logic of the dominating swarm,
the way it left the punctured globes upon the boughs.
We played a spray of ditties in his wake. They sounded like

most pickers (those in tempo; those articulating their misfortunes).
Or at least that's what I imagined going on. Black dots spread,
black spots. Pretty soon the world is one great gall. Then what?
Then we hide in the meadow. Oh, how it hums, this meadow.

BRASS

Joy Williams

Mother comes back one evening and she starts up at supper about feng shui, how our house isn't organized for a happy life, how the front door should never line up with the back door like ours does – never. One of her colleagues in Parks and Recreation told her that.

They're all dipshits down there, I said.

And the boy said, talking with his mouth full like he always does, That's why you're not supposed to have a crucifix in the bedroom. Is a cross the same as a crucifix? he says.

I could see the meat with the ketchup on it in his mouth. No, I said. A crucifix is a cross with the body on it.

A cross is OK then, he said. And a crucifix is OK as long as the eyes aren't open. You don't want that in the bedroom.

Usually nobody said anything at supper but sometimes it would go all haywire like this. I went into the backyard for a cigarette. I've got a couple of grapefruit trees that don't look so good back there, a velvet mesquite and two saguaros. All of this was here when I bought the place in 1972. The saguaros still don't have arms on them yet. A saguaro has to be seventy-five years old before it puts out an arm.

Another night, I come out of my shop in the garage for supper and he appears without a hair on his head. Not on his arms either.

Jesus, I say. What have you done now?

This is how you foil the drug testers, he says.

You aren't ingesting drugs, are you, I say.

Nah, he says. It's just unconstitutional to take a sample from a man's head, from a hair. I'm protesting the unconstitutionality of it.

As a little kid when he wanted to curse but didn't dare or probably didn't even know how, he'd say Babies! It was pretty damn cute. Oh, babies! he'd say. I don't know where he got that from.

Did he respect his mother? I'd say yes. I mean, he didn't pay much attention to her.

I fixed clocks in the garage for a while but then I stopped serving the public who were never, ever satisfied. So it's just a personal hobby, taking apart clocks and watches and putting them back together again. There was a Frenchman centuries ago, a watchmaker, who created a life-sized mechanical duck. It could move its head, flap its wings, even eat from a bowl of grain. Then it could even shit out the compacted grain. It was all gears and springs. Over four hundred parts moved each wing. They call things like that automatons.

The boy says, Can you learn about ducks by studying mechanical ducks?

Of course not, I say. No wonder his teachers don't like him, I think.

It is not a dumb question, he says, given where we are today, studying all these computer systems and simulations and making all these performance assessments which are no more than abstractions we try to apply to the real world. Real people are complex. A real situation can't be broken down into abstractions. I don't support nuclear power because there's no place to bury nuclear waste, he says. Nuclear power cannot be separated from nuclear waste.

I thought, this boy just needs to get laid, but I just said, Why are you worrying about nuclear waste, you should just go out and get a job and keep it, make some money for yourself. But I don't have a job and haven't for years so my words ring somewhat hollow. Mother has a job which is sufficient for us. There's a preacher says a family of four can live handsomely on fifty thousand dollars a year before taxes and if they make more they should give that amount away to others. And we're just a family of three. Do they still call people like us a nuclear family?

We went to New York City once. To this day I don't know why she insisted on it. Why don't we go to the Grand Canyon? I said, but she wanted to do something different. We'd seen the Grand Canyon. She wanted to go to that restaurant, Windows on the World, was it? And she wanted to take in some musical theatre. That's exactly how she put it, I want to take in some musical theatre. She's had a job for years with P&R, working with heavy machinery, loppers and saws and stuff, and first thing at LaGuardia she falls on the moving walkway and sprains her ankle. It's all she can do to hobble from bed to bathroom in the crummy little hotel room we have. So I'm supposed to be showing the boy New York City. He was around nine. We had just emerged from a subway, the boy and I, totally disoriented, and this Mexican guy passes by and grunts at me and lifts his chin at this woman standing beside us waiting for the light to change and she's blind with dark glasses and a cane, clearly blind, and the guy is saying, Do your duty, man, I'm going the other way.

The blind don't grab on to you like you'd think or clutch your hand. She just put her finger on my jacket with the lightest touch.

There's a big grate here, I said, thinking the last thing we needed was for her to get her stick snapped off in one of the holes in the grate. We cross the street and she angles herself to cross another one and I say, Do you want us to stay with you for this one as well, and she says, Thank you very much but only if you're going in this direction of course. She had the lightest, nicest, most refined voice. It was surprising. And then the boy bawls out, We don't know where we are and we don't know where we're going! And she says, still in that lovely voice, Oh, now you're beginning to frighten me. Well, I was furious at him, very, very furious. We ushered the lady across the street and then I dragged him back down into the subway and we went back uptown to the hotel and we stayed there for two days. I was the only one who went out and that was just for crackers and Coke. The boy kept saying, I'm sorry, Daddy, I'm sorry. That was what he'd do. He'd do something, give somebody he shouldn't some lip and then back right down. We didn't see anything of New York City and that was the last time we left Arizona.

I go into the bird-food store for suet. I've got some suet feeders I made. The cheaper stuff you buy in the big-box places and the hardware stores isn't rendered and can spoil. Most people don't know this. They're the same ones still putting that red dye shit in the hummingbird feeders. Every time I go in there someone's saying . . . What you got that will keep the doves away . . . I don't want the doves . . . how can I get rid of the doves . . . And the clerk is fussing around trying to sell them some contraption made from recycled materials for fifty bucks that only birds who feed upside down can get at. So I say, one customer to another, A taser. Try a taser. And they look at me sort of interested until I finally say, I'm kidding.

He found a dog out by the Raytheon plant and brought her home. She looked like a puppy but who knows. Her teeth weren't particularly white. He called her Vega.

What the hell does that mean, I say. How did you come up with that?

It's Arabic, he says.

You're just asking for trouble, aren't you, I say. Why would you give a dog an Arab's name? It doesn't even sound Arabic, it sounds Spanish. What's it in Spanish?

Open plain, he says.

That is some stupid name for a dog, I say. Open plain.

I called her Amy which didn't seem to confuse her. He stopped caring for her after a few weeks anyway and I fed her and trained her a bit. I had the time, not working. And you've got to have time, God knows, with the training exercises.

Sit . . . sit . . . good girl . . . stay . . . no! . . . sit . . . stay . . . stay . . . good girl . . . OK! Twenty minutes, twice a day.

We got all the way up to Day Fifteen, which is pretty much the end of it. That's when you get them to sit and stay and you disappear and say hello to an imaginary person at the door and you come back and then disappear again and talk to people who aren't there. That was amusing to me because no one ever came to our door, which was the way I preferred it. Sometimes the boy would have a friend over but not often. Kids, they're in a different lane. Slow. They move slow, they talk slow. Everything slows down.

The boy says, What's the point of training that dog so? She's not even good-looking.

It's true, Amy wouldn't turn any heads. And I say to him, What do you know about good-looking? Clean up that goddamned acne, boy, I wanted to say, for I can be petty with him at times, but I didn't.

A man doesn't have to be good-looking, he says, he's just got to have presence, he's just got to be in command.

Absolutely, I say. You're really in command at all the fast-food joints you keep getting fired from. He'd been fired from one for eating salad back in the kitchen with his fingers, right out of one of those bowls big as an engine block. His fingers.

It'd have been the same if I used a fork, he said.

Then the next place he'd told the manager she was sitting on her brains.

I like Amy, he said. I was the one who found her, remember.

Backing right down like he always did.

Sometimes Mother wants to make something special for dinner, like a soup. She asks me to go to Safeway and get a can of coconut milk and some cilantro. I can't imagine a worse-sounding soup but if she's willing to make dinner, I'll eat it. I'm not about to make dinner. So Amy and I drive over to the Safeway. The Brownies are out front at a little table selling cookies. They've always got somebody out front selling something, original oil paintings sometimes. Sometimes even politicians set up shop there. So I bought a box of cookies. You'd have to be some sort of wicked not to buy cookies from a little Brownie when confronted. Of course I can't find the damn coconut milk and I'm wandering around until some kid says, Can I help you, sir? and then ushers me smugly to the proper shelf. I'm going through the checkout and the checker says, Do you need any help out with this, sir?

Do you need any help out with this, sir, do you need any help out with this, sir, I mutter all the way back to the truck.

They're all automatons.

He took a poetry class at the community college. That's lovely, I say. It's quite beyond lovely, I say, sarcastic.

We're studying Rimbaud, he says. He was French, too, like your watchmaker, the one who made the duck. Isn't that interesting?

Why is that interesting, I say.

Listen to this, listen, he says. He opens up this little paperback book and he's highlighted these lines in blue Magic Marker.

He says: *For I is someone else. If brass wakes up a trumpet, it isn't to blame. To me this is evident: I give a stroke of the bow: the symphony begins to stir in the depths.*

That ain't even grammatical, I say.

For I is someone else, he says sombrely. If brass wakes up a trumpet it isn't to blame. Then he smirks at me. He's been working on this smirk.

Now that's the translation, he says. But for class I'm going to translate the translation.

Somebody should translate you, I say.

No one's going to be able to translate me, he says.

He said some old woman came in to tutor them sometimes and she smelled like laundry.

Laundry, I said. Clean laundry, I hope.

Yeah, yeah, yeah, he said.

You shouldn't need tutoring now, should you? You're in college, community college, you've been years going there.

She's one of those do-gooders. I told her about Rimbaud and she said he was the first modernist.

What the hell's that mean?

The beginning of the way we are? He was a savage dreamer, Rimbaud. And he delivers that smirk.

D addy, he says, you don't think I can do anything. I'm not going to engage you on that one, I say. You'll make your mark or you won't.

What you're wanting to do is stop time and that's dangerous, he says.

I don't want to stop time, I say. Time don't stop because I'm working on a broken watch.

But he looks at me as though he thinks it does.

I see things in parts, too, he says.

Don't you need to be wearing a cleaner shirt?

Do you think I do?

That one's filthy. I've been looking at it for days.

Are you thinking other stuff when you think that?

Godallmighty, I say. Just go put on a fresh T-shirt.

When I think something it rethinks it for me, he says.

W e've got to be tolerant, Mother says to me. You're not a tolerant man and that hurts, that shows.

Tolerant, I say. I don't know when I got into the habit of repeating a single word. Just picking it out of her conversation.

He might be neuroatypical, that's what Tom says.

They all annoy the hell out of me over at P&R but Tom takes the cake. He's so fat that I don't know how he can tie his goddamn shoes.

Tom says neurodiversity might be more crucial for the human race than biodiversity.

I say Tom's handling too much weedkiller. He's not a friend of the earth, I say. Which reminds me of something the boy lobbed at us the other night about Albert Einstein's last words. He's staring off to the side of us as we're sitting in what he loves to refer to emphatically as the *living* room and he says, Albert Einstein's last words were: Is the earth friendly?

I say, I doubt that.

Yeah, yeah, yeah, he says. It's so. I think of what I'm going to have for last words sometimes.

Let's hear 'em, I say.

It's not going to be a question.

I can't imagine your last words being a question, I say.

He looks up at me quick and decides to be pleased. Usually he won't look at a person direct. He says eye contact is counter-productive to comprehension and communication. He's got any number of ways to justify himself, that's for sure.

Mother continues to go on about Tom and Jimmy and Christina and their theories about the boy whom they've never met but think they know from her going on and on about him, I guess. She's got quite a little socializing network going on for her down at the park. She had a chance to work over at Sweetwater, the built marsh they've got out by the sewer treatment plant. She would have made more money but she said she'd be lonely with new people. She didn't want to leave her friends. She don't like change.

Neurotypical, I say. Kindly tell me what the hell TomTom is talking about. I call him that because two normal-sized men could fit in his bulk.

Neuro-*a*-typical, she says.

Oh, goodness, pardon me, I say. And why exactly are you discussing our family with those dipshits? Our family is no concern of theirs. TomTom's living with one of those little women that look like a man, isn't he? Let him worry about the atypicality of that.

She's sweet, Mother says. And anyway Tom wasn't saying anything bad about him. He was just trying to make me feel better. I told my friends about them not letting him back in those classes he was taking.

I don't want you talking to them about the boy, I say. And I want to remind you, you're the one who wanted one, not me. Just one, you said. One and done.

You're the low-hanging fruit, he says to me and Mother. She just purses her lips and pushes her fork around a serving of store-bought pie.

And I suppose you're not, I say. You're the high-hanging fruit.

You've just got to find him hilarious sometimes.

They've used up what's easy like you. They've just used you up. But now they're going to have to deal with the likes of me. And there's no formula.

The likes of you, I say.

He stands up so fast he knocks his glass of milk off the table. But then he catches it. It was flying laterally for an instant and damn if he didn't catch it. But then he storms out of the house and Mother tears up. Then the phone rings and it's one of those robo-calls you can't shut off until they've said their piece.

It was around eleven in the morning. A beautiful desert day. You forget how pretty the sky can still be. Mother was over at the park fixing a sprinkler system for the fortieth time. I think they break them deliberate so they'll have something to do. I'm in my shop thinking like I frequently do that the third cup of coffee tastes funny when all hell breaks loose. People banging on the door and screaming and shouting and I even hear a helicopter overhead. And I say, Stay, Amy, stay, and walk out of the garage and there's law officers out there screaming, *sumabitch, sumabitch* and *the Congresswoman* and *sumabitch* again, even the women, all of them in uniform and with guns, and I think whatever I was thinking a minute ago is the last peaceful thought I will ever have. Though sometimes now I try to pretend he's still in the house, in his room with the door closed. I pretend he's still living with us and eating with us and getting by with us. But of course he's not and he isn't.

No, we were never afraid of him. Afraid of Jared? ∎

GRANTA

'A witty noir *Don Quixote* ... a blackly comic fable about emptiness, loneliness and the hollow lure of gold' – *Financial Times*

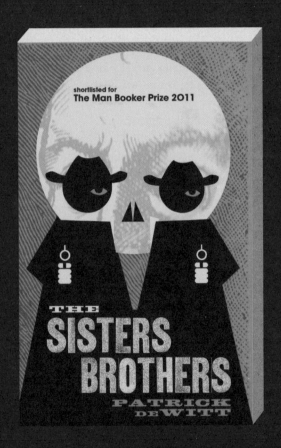

A dazzlingly original and darkly funny offbeat western about a reluctant assassin and his murderous brother.

GRANTABOOKS.COM

Give the gift
of new writing

Buy a gift subscription to *Granta*
and save over 40% off the cover price

'An indispensable part of the intellectual landscape'
– *Observer*

UK
£34.95
(£29.95 by Direct Debit)

EUROPE
£39.95

REST OF THE WORLD*
£45.95

Subscribe now by completing the form overleaf, visiting granta.com
or calling free phone 0500 004 033

* Not for people in US, Canada or Latin America
– there's one of these cards just for you a bit further on . . .

GRANTA.COM

GRANTA

THE MAGAZINE OF NEW WRITING

SUBSCRIPTION FORM FOR UK, EUROPE AND REST OF THE WORLD

Yes, I would like to take out a subscription to *Granta*.

GUARANTEE: If I am ever dissatisfied with my *Granta* subscription, I will simply notify you, and you will send me a complete refund or credit my credit card, as applicable, for all un-mailed issues.

YOUR DETAILS	GIFT RECIPIENT DETAILS
MR / MISS / MRS / DR	MR / MISS / MRS / DR ....
NAME	NAME ....
ADDRESS	ADDRESS ....
....	....
POSTCODE	POSTCODE ....
EMAIL	EMAIL ....

(Only provide your email if you are happy for Granta *to communicate with you this way)*

☐ Please tick this box if you do not wish to receive special offers from *Granta*
☐ Please tick this box if you do not wish to receive offers from organizations selected by *Granta*

YOUR PAYMENT DETAILS

1) ☐ Pay £29.95 (saving £22) by Direct Debit
To pay by Direct Debit please complete the mandate below and return to the address shown below.

2) Pay by cheque or credit/debit card. Please complete below:

1 year subscription: ☐ UK: £34.95 ☐ Europe: £39.95 ☐ Rest of World: £45.95

3 year subscription: ☐ UK: £89.95 ☐ Europe: £99 ☐ Rest of World: £122

I wish to pay by ☐ CHEQUE ☐ CREDIT/DEBIT CARD
Cheque enclosed for £ _____ made payable to *Granta*.

Please charge £ _____ to my: ☐ Visa ☐ Mastercard ☐ Amex ☐ Switch/Maestro ☐ Issue No.
Card No. ☐☐☐☐☐☐☐☐☐☐☐☐☐☐☐☐

Valid from *(if applicable)* ☐☐☐☐   Expiry Date ☐☐☐☐
Security No. ☐☐☐☐

SIGNATURE .... DATE ....

Instructions to your Bank or Building Society to pay by Direct Debit
BANK NAME ....
BANK ADDRESS ....
POSTCODE ....
ACCOUNT IN THE NAMES(S) OF: ....
SIGNED ....
DATE ....

DIRECT Debit

Instructions to your Bank or Building Society: Please pay Granta Publications direct debits from the account detailed on this instruction subject to the safeguards assured by the direct debit guarantee. I understand that this instruction may remain with Granta and, if so, details will be passed electronically to my bank/building society. Banks and building societies may not accept direct debit instructions from some types of account.

Bank/building society account number
☐☐☐☐☐☐☐☐

Sort Code
☐☐☐☐☐☐☐☐

Originator's Identification
☐9☐1☐3☐1☐3☐3

Please mail this order form with payment instructions to:

Granta Publications
12 Addison Avenue
London, W11 4QR
Or call 0500 004 033
or visit GRANTA.COM

THE
STARVELING

Don DeLillo

When it started, long before the woman, he lived in one room. He did not hope for improved circumstances. This was where he belonged, single window, shower, hotplate, a squat refrigerator parked in the bathroom, a makeshift closet for scant possessions. There is a kind of uneventfulness that resembles meditation. One morning he sat drinking coffee and staring into space when the lamp that extended from the wall rustled into flame. Faulty wiring, he thought calmly, and put out his cigarette. He watched the flames rise, the lampshade begin to bubble and melt. The memory ended here.

Now, decades later, he sat watching another woman, the one he lived with. She was at the kitchen sink, washing her cereal bowl, using a soapy bare hand to scour the edges. They were divorced now, after five or six years of marriage, still sharing an apartment, hers, a third-floor walk-up, sufficient space, sort of, tiny barking dog next door.

She was still lean, Flory, and a little lopsided, the soft brownish-blonde tones only now beginning to fade from her hair. One of her brassieres hung from the doorknob on the closet. He looked at it, wondering how long it had been there. It was a life that had slowly grown around them, unfailingly familiar, and there was nothing much to see that had not been seen in previous hours, days, weeks and months. The brassiere on the doorknob was a matter of months, he thought.

He sat on his cot at the other end of the narrow flat, listening to her talk idly about her new job, temporary, doing traffic reports on the radio. She was an actor, occupationally out of work, and took

what came her way. Hers was the only living voice he attended to in
the course of most days, an easy sort of liquid cadence with a trace of
Deep South. But her broadcast voice was a power tool, all bursts and
breathless medleys, and when it was possible, when he happened to
be here, which was rare, during the daylight hours, he turned on the
radio and listened to the all-news station where she had a narrow slot
every eleven minutes, reporting on the routine havoc out there.

She spoke fantastically fast, words and key phrases expertly
compressed into coded format, the accidents, road repairs, bridges
and tunnels, the delays measured in geologic time. The BQE, the
FDR, always the biblical Cross Bronx, ten thousand drivers with
deadened eyes waiting for the gates to open, the seas to part.

He watched her approach now, slantwise, her body language of
determined inquiry, head flopped left, eyes advancing through levels
of scrutiny. She stopped at a distance of five feet.

'Did you get a haircut?'

He sat thinking, then reached back to run his thumb over the back
of his neck. A haircut was a hurried few moments in a well-scheduled
day, submitted to in order to be forgotten.

'I think so, absolutely.'

'When?'

'I don't know. Maybe three days ago.'

She took a step to the side, approaching once again.

'What's wrong with me? I'm just now noticing,' she said. 'What
did he do to you?'

'Who?'

'The barber.'

'I don't know. What did he do to me?'

'He emasculated your sideburns,' she said.

She touched the side of his head, honouring the memory, it
seemed, of what had been there, her hand still wet from the cereal
bowl. Then she danced away, into a jacket and out the door. This is
what they did, they came and went. She had to hurry to the studio, in
midtown, and he had a movie to get to, 10.40 a.m., walking distance

from here, and then another movie somewhere else, and somewhere else after that, and then one more time before his day was done.

It was a slow white summer day and there were men in orange vests jackhammering along the middle of the broad street, with concrete barriers rimming the raw crevice and every moving thing on either side taking defensive measures, taxis in stop-and-start pattern and pedestrians sprinting across the street in stages, in tactical bursts, cell-phones welded to their heads.

He walked west, beginning to feel the flesh in his step, the width of chest and hips. He'd always been big, slow and strong and he was bigger and slower now, all those fistfuls of saturated fat that he pushed into his face, helplessly, sitting slumped over the counter in diners or standing alongside food carts. He didn't eat meals, he grabbed meals, he grabbed a bite and paid and fled, and the aftertaste of whatever he absorbed lingered for hours somewhere in the lower tracts.

This was his father eating, the ageing son assuming the father's spacious frame, if nothing else.

He turned north on Sixth Avenue, knowing that the theatre would be near empty, three or four solitary souls. Moviegoers were souls when there were only a few of them. This was almost always the case late morning or early afternoon. They would remain solitary even as they left the theatre, not exchanging a word or glance, unlike souls in the course of other kinds of witness, a remote accident or threat of nature.

He paid at the booth, got his ticket, gave it to the man in the lobby and went directly to the catacomb toilets. A few minutes later he took his seat in the small theatre and waited for the feature to begin. Wait now, hurry later, these were the rules of the day. Days were all the same, movies were not.

His name was Leo Zhelezniak. It took half a lifetime before he began to fit into the name. Did he think there was a resonance in the name, or a foreignness, a history, that he could never earn? Other people lived in their names. He used to wonder whether the name itself made any difference. Maybe he would feel this separation no matter what name he carried on the plastic cards in his wallet.

He had the row to himself, seated dead centre as the house went dark. Whatever moons of disquiet and melancholy hovered over his experience, recent or distant, this was the place where it might all evaporate.

Flory had ideas about his vocation. In those early years, between acting jobs, voice-overs, sales fairs and dog-walking, she occasionally joined him, three movies some days, even four, the novelty of it, the sort of inspired lunacy. A film can be undermined by the person you're seeing it with, there in the dark, a ripple effect of attitude, scene by scene, shot by shot. They both knew this. They also knew that she would do nothing to compromise the integrity of his endeavour – no whispers, nudges, bags of popcorn. But she did not overplay her sense of careful forethought. She was not a trite person. She understood that he was not turning a routine diversion into some hellish obsession.

What, then, was he doing?

She advanced theories. He was an ascetic, she said. This was one theory. She found something saintly and crazed in his undertaking, an element of self-denial, an element of penance. Sit in the dark, revere the images. Were his parents Catholic? Did his grandparents go to Mass every day, before first light, in some village in the Carpathian Mountains, repeating the words of a priest with a long white beard and golden cloak? Where *were* the Carpathian Mountains? She spoke late at night, usually in bed, bodies at rest, and he liked listening to these ideas. They were impeccable fictions, with no attempt on her part to get his rendering of what might be the case. Maybe she knew it would have to be dredged out of his pores, a fever in the skin rather than a product of conscious mind.

Or he was a man escaping his past. He needed to dream away a grim memory of childhood, some misadventure of adolescence. Movies are waking dreams – daydreams, she said, protection against the recoil of that early curse, that bane. She seemed to be speaking lines from the misbegotten revival of a once-loved play. The tender sound of her voice, the make-believe she was able to unfurl, sometimes distracted Leo, who'd feel an erection beginning to hum beneath the sheets.

Was he at the movies to see a movie, she said, or maybe more narrowly, more essentially, simply to be at the movies?

He thought about this.

He could stay home and watch TV, movie after movie, on cable, three hundred channels, she said, deep into the night. He wouldn't have to get from theatre to theatre, subways, buses, worry, rush, and he'd be far more comfortable, he'd save himself money, he'd eat half-decent meals.

He thought about this. It was obvious, wasn't it, that there were simpler alternatives. Every alternative was simpler. A job was simpler. Dying was simpler. But he understood that her question was philosophical, not practical. She was probing his deeper recesses. Being at the movies to be at the movies. He thought about this. He owed her the gesture.

The woman entered as the feature began. He hadn't seen her in a while and was surprised to realize, only now, that he'd noted her absence. She was a recent enlistee – is that the word? He wasn't sure when she'd started showing up. She seemed awkward, slightly angular, and she was far younger than the others. There were others, the floating group of four or five people who made the circuit every day, each keeping to his or her rigid schedule, criss-crossing the city, theatre to theatre, mornings, nights, weekends, years.

Leo did not count himself part of the group. He did not speak to the others, ever, not a word, not a look directed their way. He saw them nonetheless, now and then, here and there, one or the other. They were vague shapes with pasty faces, planted among the lobby posters in their weary clothing, restless bearing, their post-operative posture.

He tried not to care that there were others. But how could it fail to disturb him? The sightings were unavoidable, one person at the Quad, another the next day at the Sunshine, two of them at Empire 25 in the vast rotunda or on the long steep narrow escalator that seems to lead to some high-rise form of hell.

But this was different, she was different, and he was watching her. She was seated two rows in front of him, end of the row, with the first images bringing pale light to the front of the house.

There was the long metal bar of the old police lock set into its floor niche inches from the front door. There was the tall narrow radiator, a relic, unscreened, with a pan set beneath the shut-off valve to collect the drip. At times he stared into the columns of the radiator, thinking whatever he was thinking, none of it reducible to words.

There was the cramped bathroom they shared, where his broad bottom could barely wedge itself between the tub and the wall and onto the toilet seat.

Sometimes he left his cot, by invitation, and spent the night with Flory in her bedroom, where they had wistful sex. She had a boyfriend, Avner, but said nothing about him beyond the name itself and the fact that he had a son living in Washington.

There was the photograph of her grandmother and grandfather on one wall, the kind of old family photo so drained of colour and tone that it is generic, somebody's forebears, ancestors, dead relatives.

There were the notebooks crammed into the back of the closet, Leo's composition books, reminiscent of grade school, the black-and-white mottled covers, the marbled covers. These were his notes, years and miles of scrawled testimony that he'd once compiled about the movies he saw. Name of theatre, title of film, starting time, running time, random thoughts on plot, principals, scenes and whatever else occurred to him – the talky teenagers seated nearby and what he said to shut them up, or the way the white subtitles disappeared into white backgrounds, stranding him with a raging argument in Korean or Farsi.

In bed with her, he sometimes flashed a thought of Avner in some dark shrouded shape-changing form, a moonless presence hovering in the room.

Flory liked to punch him in the stomach, for fun. He tried to find the humour in it. Often, late, he'd come home to find her kickboxing in her pyjamas. This was part of a regimen that included diet, stylized movement and lengthy meditation, her body face up on the floor, a dish towel over her eyes. She did summer stock, gone for weeks, and sometimes, his senses dulled down, he barely knew that he was alone in the apartment.

There was his face in the mirror, gradually becoming asymmetrical, features no longer on the same axis, brows unaligned, jaw crooked, his mouth slightly aslant.

When did this begin to happen? What happens next?

They lived on nearly nothing, his wilted savings and her occasional flurries of work. They lived on habit, occupying long silences that were never tense or self-conscious. Other times, studying a playscript, she paced the floor, trying out voices, and he listened without comment. She used to give him haircuts but then stopped.

When she forgot something she wanted to tell him, she went to wherever the thought had originated, kitchen, bathroom, bedroom, and waited for it to recur.

There was a bottle of Polish vodka resting on top of the ice trays in the refrigerator. He might ignore it for three months and then, one midnight, drink sippingly and methodically from a water glass, lying back on the cot an hour later with the world all closed down, nothing left of it but a terminal throbbing ache in his forebrain.

There were the traffic reports, the sound of Flory's voice pressurized into twenty-five seconds of gridlock alerts, lane closings, emergency guardrail repairs. He sat hunched by the radio listening for hints of total global collapse in the news of a flipped vehicle on the inbound Gowanus. These reports were the Yiddish slang of everything gone wrong, reformulated in the speed diction and cool command of her delivery.

There was the fact that she'd never appeared in a movie, not as a walk-on, not in a crowd scene, and he wondered if somehow, secretly, she blamed him.

There were all the things they lived with, plain objects strangely charged with shaping their reality, things touched but not seen, or seen through.

He spent a year in college in his late twenties, working nights at the main post office on Eighth Avenue, and he took a course in philosophy that he looked forward to, week by week, page by page, mining even the footnotes in the text. Then it got hard and he stopped.

If we're not here to know what a thing is, then what is it?

There was her brassiere dangling from the doorknob on the closet.

He thought, What is it?

He left his seat while the final credits were rolling, an action he took only when the day's schedule was extremely tight. This wasn't the case today. He went out onto the avenue and stood near the kerbstone. He faced the theatre and waited. A man passed by, putting on lip balm, and this made Leo look up to check the position of the sun.

It wasn't long before the young woman emerged. She wore jeans tucked into dark boots and looked different in bright light, whiter, thinner, he wasn't sure. She paused for a moment, people skimming past. He thought she also looked worried and then he thought it wasn't worry but only a basic alertness to the essential details, the next showtime, the quickest way to get there. She wore a loose grey shirt and carried a shoulder bag.

Cabs went blasting past behind him.

She began to move away, long brown hair, long slow deliberate strides, tight ass in those faded jeans. He figured she was headed to the subway entrance north of here. He stood in place for an extended moment, then found himself walking in the same direction, following. Was he following? Did he need someone to tell him what he was doing? Did he need to check his position in the solar system because he'd seen a man applying sunscreen to his lips?

The next movie in his day was diagonally crosstown, up on East Eighty-Sixth Street, but he could take the A train here, if the situation warranted, and then make his way across the park by bus. Built into his code of daily travel was the conviction never to take taxis. A taxi seemed like cheating, even if he wasn't sure exactly what this meant. But he knew what money meant, the tactile fact of cash leaving the hand – folding money, rubbed coins.

He moved into a trot now, already reaching for his transit card. She was still in sight, barely, among the sidewalk swarm. He had the transit card in his breast pocket, the day's slate written on an index card in the opposite pocket. He had his loose change, wallet, house keys, handkerchief, all the ordinary items that established the vital identity of his days. There was his hunger to be considered, food, soon, to steel the sorry body. He had the old Seiko wristwatch with the frayed leather band.

He paid careful attention to rain in movies. In foreign films, set in northern or eastern Europe, it seemed, sometimes, to be raining God or raining death.

Sometimes, also, he imagined himself being foreign, walking stooped and unshaven along the sides of buildings, although he didn't know why this seemed foreign. He could see himself in another life, some nameless city in Belarus or Romania. The Romanians made impressive films. Flory read movie reviews, sometimes aloud. Foreign directors were often called masters, the Taiwanese master, the Iranian master. She said you had to be a foreigner to be a master. He saw himself walking past cafes in black-and-white cities, with trolley cars going past, and lipsticked women in pretty dresses. These visions would fade in seconds but in a curious way, a serious way, they had the density of a lifetime compressed.

Flory thought he did not have to imagine an alternative life as a foreigner. He was actually leading an alternative life. In the real life, she said, he is a schoolteacher in one of the outer boroughs, a run-down neighbourhood. Late one afternoon he and his colleagues get together in a local bar and describe the lives they might be living under different circumstances. Fake lives, joke lives, but on the margins of plausibility. After several drinks it is a bleary Leo who proposes the most reckless life. It is this life, his life, the movies. The others wave him off. Leo least of all, they say. The man is too earthbound, pragmatic, the most literal-minded of the bunch.

She brought the story around to their third-floor walk-up, the sight of him at the other end of the flat, seated on his cot, lacing his shoes. This is why they were still living together, she said. His stolid nature was her bedrock. She needed only what there was in plain sight, this man in body, in careless bulk, his gravitational force keeping her in balance.

Otherwise she was windblown, unfixed, eating and sleeping sporadically, never getting around to things. The rent, the phone bill, the leak, the rot, all the things you have to get around to, all the time, before they find you dead in your grandmother's nightgown. Leo did not go to the doctor but she went to the doctor because he did not. She filled prescriptions because he was here, sweeping the floor and taking out the garbage. He was not springloaded, he was safe. There was no explosion in that crouched form.

Years later people can't remember why they got married. Leo couldn't remember why they divorced. It had something to do with Flory's world view. She dropped out of the neighbourhood association, the local acting company, the volunteers for the homeless. Then she stopped voting, stopped eating meat and stopped being married. She devoted more time to her stabilization exercises, training herself to maintain difficult body positions, draped over a chair, rolled into a dense mass on the floor, a bolus, motionless for long periods, seemingly unaware of anything beyond her abdominal muscles, her vertebrae. To Leo she seemed nearly swallowed by her surroundings, on the verge of melting out of sight, dematerializing.

He watched her and thought of something he'd heard or read years earlier, in philosophy class.

All human existence is a trick of light.

He tried to recall the context of the remark. Was it about the universe and our remote and fleeting place as earthlings? Or was it something much more intimate, people in rooms, what we see and what we miss, how we pass through each other, year by year, second by second?

They'd stopped speaking to each other in meaningful ways, she said, and they'd stopped having meaningful sex.

But they needed to be here, each with the other, and he finished lacing his shoes and then stood and turned and raised the shade. The slat jutted slightly from its hem and he tried to decide whether to nudge it back into place or leave it as it was, at least for now. He remained a moment, facing the window, scarcely aware of the noise of traffic from the street.

This is where he spent part of nearly every day, ordinary rider, standing man, the subway, his back to the door. He and others, lives at pause, faces emptied out, and she as well, seated near the end of the car. He didn't have to look directly at her. There she was, head down, knees tight, upper body swivelled toward the bulkhead.

This was the midday lull between the breathless edges of the rush hours but she sat as if enclosed by others and he thought she was still getting used to the subway. He thought a number of things. He thought she was a person who lived within herself, remote, elusive, whatever else. Her gaze was down and away, into nothing. He scanned the ad panels above the windows, reading the Spanish copy over and over. She had no friends, one friend. This is how he chose to define her, for now, in the early stages.

The train pulled into a station, Forty-Second Street, Port Authority, and he stood away from the door and waited. She didn't move, didn't budge, and he began to imagine a crowded car, both of them standing, his body jammed against hers, pressed into her. Which way is she facing? She is facing away from him, they are front to back, bodies guided by the swerves and changing speeds, train racing past stations now, an unscheduled express.

He needed to stop thinking for a while. Or is this what everybody needed? Everybody here with eyes averted thinking about everybody else in whatever unknowable way, a total cross-current of feelings, wishes, dim imaginings, one second to the next.

There was a word he wanted to apply to her. It was a medical or psychological term and it took a long moment before he was able to think of it, *anorexic*, one of those words that carries its meaning with a vengeance. But it was too extreme for her. She wasn't that thin, she wasn't gaunt, she wasn't even young enough to be one, an anorectic. Did he know why he was doing this, any of it, from the instant he decided to take the wrong train, her train? There was nothing to know. It was minute-to-minute, see what's next.

Soon he was following her along the street and out of the heat and noise of this stretch of Broadway into the cool columned lobby of a major multiplex. She went past the automated ticket machines and approached the counter at the far end of the lobby. Posters everywhere, a bare scatter of people. She stepped onto the escalator and he understood that he could not lose sight of her now. He rode up toward the huge Hollywood mural and onto the carpeted second floor. There was a man on a sofa reading a book. She went past the video-game consoles and handed her ticket to the woman stationed at the entrance to the theatres.

All these elements, seemingly connected, here to there, step by step, but with no thought in his mind of a purposeful end – just the unfixed rhythm of his need.

He stood at the access point, able to see her enter Theatre 6. He went back to the lobby and asked for a ticket to whatever was showing there. The ticket seller tapped it out, deadpan, and he headed to the escalator, walking past the security guard whose nonchalance was probably genuine. On the second floor again he handed the ticket to the uniformed woman and walked past the long food counter, veering into Theatre 6. Roughly two dozen heads in the semi-dark. He scanned the seats and found her, fifth row, far end.

There was no satisfaction in this, having tracked her from the end of one movie to the start of another. He felt only that a requirement had been met, the easing of an indistinct tension. He was halfway down the side aisle when he decided to sit directly behind her. The impulse took him by surprise and he moved into the seat tentatively, needing to adjust to the blatant fact of being there. Then the screen lit up and the previews came at them like forms of laboratory torture, in swift image and high pitch.

Their bodies were aligned, eyes aligned, his and hers. But the movie was hers, her film, her theatre, and he wasn't prepared for the confusion. The movie seemed stillborn. He could not absorb what was happening. He sat with legs spread, knees braced against the seat in front of him. He was practically breathing on her and this proximity helped him work his way into things that hadn't been clear up to now. She was a woman alone. This had to be the case. She lives alone, in one room, as he did. Those were years that still gathered force in his memory, and the choice he would make, the fact of this life, scratched-out, gouged-out, first became a vision in that room. She looks down at warped floorboards. There is no bathtub, only a shower with tinny sides that rattle if you lean on them. She forgets to bathe, forgets to eat. She lies in bed, eyes open, and replays scenes from the day's films, shot by shot. She has the capacity to do this. It is natural, it is innate. She doesn't care about the actors, only the characters. They are the ones who speak, and look sadly out of windows, and die violently.

He took his eyes off the screen. Her head and shoulders, this is what he looked at, a woman who avoids contact with others, sometimes sits in her room staring at a wall. He thinks of her as a true soul, not knowing exactly what that means. Is he sure that she doesn't live with her parents? Can she manage alone? She sees certain movies many times, unlike him. She will hunt down mythical movies, those once-in-a-decade screenings. Leo saw such films only when they drifted into view. She will devote her energies to finding and seeing the elusive masterwork, damaged print, missing footage, running time eleven hours, twelve hours, nobody seems sure, a privileged act, a blessing – you travel to London, Lisbon, Prague or maybe just Brooklyn, and you sit in a crowded room and feel transformed.

OK, he understood this. She steps away from her own shadow. She is a scant being trying to find a place to be. But there was something she had to understand. This is everyday life, this is the job, day to day. Your head is folded into a newspaper or plugged into a telephone so you can measure movie times against estimated travel times. You make the slate, keep the hours, remain true to the plan. This is what we do, he thought.

He closed his eyes for a time. He tried to see her standing naked in body profile before a mirror. She looked frail, undernourished, watching herself, half wondering who that person is. He thought about her name. He needed a name, a way to claim her, something to know her by. When he opened his eyes a house stood on-screen, alone in a wintry field. He thought of her as the Starveling. That was her name.

There was the day in Philadelphia, the day it opened, *Apocalypse Now*, over thirty years ago, the 9.20 a.m. show, the Goldman, on Fifteenth Street. He was in town because his father had just died and he was at the movies because he could not stay away, arriving at nine sharp with a criminal's conscience, his father's death and imminent funeral serving as bookends for Brando in the jungle. His father left property to a couple of loyal friends and the money went to Leo, pretty serious money, meatpacker's money, union head's money, heavy drinker, gambler, widower, a master of graft and other amenities.

Then there was the day, decades later, when Brando died. The news came over the radio. Marlon Brando dead at eighty. It didn't make sense to Leo. Brando eighty. Brando dead made more sense than Brando eighty. It was the guy in the T-shirt or tank top who was dead, the leather jacket, not the old man with the bulging cheeks and raspy voice. Later, at the supermarket, before the first screening of the day, he expected to hear people talking about it in the checkout lines but they had other matters in mind. Do I want the olive oil spray or the canola spray? Debit or credit? He stood there thinking of his father. Two deaths forever linked, and the money, his father's bequest, was the thing that allowed him eventually to leave his job at the post office and take up the life, full-time, with Flory's encouragement.

They were just getting to know each other then. He'd already started filling notebooks with facts and commentaries, personal interpretations, and she found this fascinating. Already stacks of those schoolroom notebooks, his handwriting unreadable, half a million words, a million words, film by film, day by day, building into a cultural chronicle to be discovered a hundred years from now, one man's eccentric history of an entire era. He was a serious man. This is what she loved about Leo, she said, seated on the floor smoking dope in her underwear, with black goggles wrapped around her head. The man was gripped by a passion, a total immersion that was uncompromising, and the notebooks were solid evidence of this, objects you could clutch in your hands, words you could count, the tangible truth of a monkish dedication, and the murky handwriting only added to the wonder of the enterprise, like ancient script in a lost language.

Then he stopped.

Movies of every kind, from everywhere, maps of world imagery, and then you stop?

He stopped, he said, because the notebooks had become the reason for what he was doing. What he was doing was going to the movies. The notebooks were beginning to replace the movies. The movies didn't need the movie notes. They only needed him to be there.

Is this when she stopped cutting his hair? He wasn't sure.

He'd known from the beginning that he was advancing toward a future without paydays, holidays, birthdays, new moons, full moons, real meals or very much in the way of world news. He wanted the native act, clean, free of extraneous sensation.

He never looked at ticket sellers or ticket takers. Someone handed him a ticket, he handed it back to someone else. This stayed the same, almost everything stayed the same. But now days seemed to end an hour after they started. It was always the end of the day. The days had no names and this should not have mattered. But there was something unsettling in the anonymous week, not a sense of elemental time but of time emptied out. He walked up the stairs, near midnight, and it was here and now, night after night, that he became intensely conscious of the moment, approaching the third floor, slowing his pace, wary of rousing the neighbour's rat-faced barking dog. Another end of another day. The previous day had just ended, it seemed, at this precise place on the stairway, with the same cautious footstep, and he could see himself clearly, then and now, in mid-step.

All forgotten until the following night, when the same feeling occurred, at the same place, one step from the landing.

First there was the crosstown bus and then the subway, 6 train, uptown. He thought they were headed to a theatre on the Upper East Side. He also thought there had to be another word, beyond *anorexic*, that would help him see her clearly, a word invented for certain individuals to aspire to, as if they were born and raised to wrap themselves inside it.

He watched her, half a car away.

She almost never speaks. When she speaks, is there a stutter, an accent? An accent might be interesting, somewhere Scandinavian, but he decided he didn't want one. She has no telephone. She forgets to shop – food, shoes, toiletries – or simply rejects the notion. She hears voices, she hears dialogue from movies she saw as a child.

She remained in her seat when they reached Eighty-Sixth Street. This made him nervous and he began to count the stops now. When he reached an even dozen the train made a leap into daylight and he found himself scanning a scene of tenements, housing projects, jagged streaks of rooftop graffiti and a river or inlet he could not identify.

She is also erratic, possibly self-destructive. There are times when she flings herself against the wall. It occurred to him that what he was doing made complete sense, to define her as someone who has taken this life, *their life*, to its predetermined limit. She has no recourse to sensible measures. She is pure, he is not. Does she forget her name? Is it possible for her to imagine the slightest semblance of well-being?

He checked the street names on the electronic route map across the aisle, dots blinking off, one by one, Whitlock, Elder, Morrison, and he began to understand where he was. He was in the Bronx, which meant he'd strayed outside the known borders. Sunlight filled the car, making him feel exposed, deprived of the cover, the protective aura he'd experienced beneath street level.

Across from him a tiny brown woman held a half-smoked cigarette, unlit. On the platform, finally, he followed the other woman, the one he was following, down to street level and along a broad avenue lined with shops, storefront offices, a Bangladeshi grocery, a Chino-Latino restaurant. He stopped noticing things and watched her walk. She seemed to be thinking each stride into physical being. They crossed the overpass of an expressway and she turned into a street of row houses with aluminium awnings. He stopped and waited for her to enter one of the houses and now the street was empty except for him.

He walked slowly back toward the train station, not knowing what to make of this. Did it contradict everything he'd come to believe about her? This street, these family homes, the difficulty she faced in getting to theatres clustered in Manhattan. In a way it made her a more compelling figure. It confirmed her determination, the depth of her calling.

She lived here because she had to live somewhere. She could not manage alone. She is staying with an older sister and her family. They are the only white family left on the block. She is the strange one, the one who never says where she is going, who rarely takes meals with the others, the one who will never marry.

Maybe there was no technical term or medical name for what she did or what she was. She just wandered on past, free of all that.

He felt the heat, Bangladeshi heat, West Indian heat. He read the names on the windows of local enterprises. This is what she sees every day, Tattoo Mayhem, Metropolitan Brace and Limb. He decided to wait within sight of the stairway to the elevated tracks. If there was a movie to come, she would show up eventually to get on the train. He ate something in Kabir's Bakery and waited, then went to Dunkin' Donuts and ate something else and waited, looking out the window. Was this the first food he'd eaten all day? Was she eating while he was eating? Did the Starveling eat?

He stood in the shadows on the corner, under the el, trains arriving and leaving, people everywhere, and he watched them, he so seldom did this, evening slowly unfolding. There was nothing here that was not ordinary but he felt compelled to examine the scene, searching for something he could not identify. Then he saw her, across the street. She was born to be unseen, he thought, except by him. She willed it, she carried it with her, the wary look and taut body, the inwardness, the void of touch. Who touched her, ever?

She wore a dark sweater now, V-neck, and there was an umbrella handle jutting from the shoulder bag.

Take the umbrella, her sister had said. Just in case.

He followed her up the stairs to the platform, same track as before, uptown, and this was another reality to absorb, that they were not headed back to Manhattan. They rode five stops to the end of the line and she went to street level and boarded a waiting bus. He felt lost and dumb, wandering blind, a passive victim of some shadowy manipulation. He also felt close to the point of breaking off contact. The bus sat there, marked Bx29. People kept boarding and after a while he followed, taking a seat near the front. Nothing happened but time seemed to be rushing past. He could see it out the window, sky darkening, things in motion. A man and woman behind him were speaking Greek. He thought the Greeks were in Queens.

Then they were moving past a landscape of parkways, thruways, loops and interchanges, and the bus entered an enormous shopping complex, several malls, more or less contiguous, national names everywhere, franchises and megastores, a hundred soaring logos, and out there, beyond, he saw the lights and regimented shapes of a great sweep of high-rise buildings.

She nearly brushed his shoulder when she got off the bus. It wasn't until he stepped out onto the sidewalk that he realized he was standing in front of a movie theatre. He stared into the transparent facade. He was ready to believe all over again. There she was inside the lobby, her sketchy body moving along the winding ticket line. He was ready to trust the moment, be himself, like a man bracingly awake after a panic dream.

He checked the display of features and starting times and bought a ticket to the film about to screen. He rode the escalator to the second level and entered Theatre 3. There she was at the end of a row near the front. He took a seat where he could in a crowded house and tried to think along with her, to feel what she was feeling.

Always the sense of anticipation. To look forward to, invariably, whatever the title, the story, the director, and to be able to elude the spectre of disappointment. There were no disappointments, ever, not for him, not for her. They were here to be enveloped, to be transcended. Something would fly past them, reaching back to take them with it.

That was the innocent surface, on loan from childhood. There was more but what was it? It was something he'd never tried to penetrate until now, the crux of being who he was and understanding why he needed this. He sensed it in her, knew it was there, the same half life. They had no other self. They had no fake self, no veneer. They could only be the one embedded thing they were, stripped of the faces that come naturally to others. They were bare-faced, bare-souled, and maybe this is why they were here, to be safe. The world was up there, framed, on the screen, edited and corrected and bound tight, and they were here, where they belonged, in the isolated dark, being what they were, being safe.

Movies take place in the dark. This seemed an obscure truth, just now stumbled upon.

It took him a moment to realize that this was the same movie he'd seen the day before, way downtown, in Battery Park. He didn't know how to feel about this. He decided not to feel stupid. What would happen when the movie ended? This is what he ought to be thinking about.

He watched it end the same way it had ended twenty-four hours ago. She remained in her seat with people shuffling past. He did the same, waiting for her to move, a full fifteen minutes. He recognized the meaning. Movie over, no wish to leave, nothing out there but heat rising from the pavement. This is where they belonged, in a tier of empty seats, no false choices. Did he want to own her, or just touch her once, hear her speak a few words? One touch might ease the need. The place smelled of seat cushions, the dust of warm bodies.

The restrooms were at the end of a corridor. The area was clearing out when she went in that direction. He stood at the head of the corridor, thinking, trying to think. There was nothing to trust but the blank mind. Maybe he felt that he was standing watch, waiting for the other women, if there were any, to come out of the restroom. He wasn't sure what he wanted to do next and then he walked down the hall and pushed open the door. She was at the washbasin farthest from the door, splashing water in her face. The shoulder bag was at her feet. She looked up and saw him. Nothing happened, neither person moved. He drifted toward a state of neutral observation. *Neither person moved,* he thought. Then he glanced at the row of stalls, all apparently empty, doors unlatched. This was a motivated act, stark and telling, and she moved away, toward the far wall.

There were gaps in the silence, a feeling of stop and go. She was looking past him. She had the face and eyes of someone distant in time, a woman in a painting, curtains hanging in loose folds. He wanted one of them to say something.

He said, 'The faucets in the men's toilet aren't working.'

This seemed incomplete.

'I came in here,' he said, 'to wash my hands.'

He didn't know what would happen next. The white glare of the toilet was deathly. He felt sweat working along his shoulders and down his back. Even if she wasn't facing him directly, he was in her sightline. What would happen if she looked at him straight on, eye to eye? Is this the contact she feared, the look that triggers the action?

Neither person moved, he thought.

He nodded to her, absurdly. Her face and hands were still wet. She stood with one arm bent in front of her but it didn't seem defensive to him. She was not fending, staving off. She was just caught in mid-motion, the other arm at her side, palm of hand flat against the wall.

He tried to imagine what he looked like to her, man of some size, some years, but what did he look like to anyone? He had no idea.

He felt a kind of tremor in his right arm. He thought it might begin shaking. He clenched his fist, just to see if he could do it. The thing to do was to make himself known, tell her who he was, for both of them to hear.

He said, 'I keep thinking of a Japanese movie I saw about ten years ago. It was sepia tone, like greyish brown, three and a half hours plus, an afternoon screening in Times Square, theatre gone now, and I can't remember the title of the movie. This should drive me crazy but it doesn't. Something happened to my memory somewhere along the way. It's because I don't sleep well. Sleep and memory are intertwined. There's a bus being hijacked, people dead, I was the only person in the theatre. The theatre was located down under a monster store selling CDs, DVDs, headsets, videocassettes, all kinds of audio equipment, and you go into the store and down some stairs and there's a movie theatre and you buy a ticket and go in. I used to know everything about every movie I ever saw but it's all fading away. It embarrasses me to say three and a half hours. I should be talking about minutes, the exact number of minutes that make up the running time.'

His voice sounded peculiar. He could hear it as though he were listening to someone else speaking. It was a steady voice, without inflection, a flat low drone.

'The lobby and theatre were both deserted. Nobody anywhere. Was there a refreshment stand? This much I remember, the experience itself, alone in this place watching a movie in a language

I don't understand, with subtitles, down under the street, eerie and tomblike, passengers dead, hijacker dead, driver survives, some kids survive. I used to know every title of every foreign film in English plus the original language. But my memory's shot. One thing doesn't change for you and me. We arrange the day, don't we? It's all compiled, it's organized, we make sense of it. And once we're in our seats and the feature begins, it's like something we always knew, over and over, but we can't really share it with others. Stanley Kubrick grew up in the Bronx but nowhere near where you live. Tony Curtis, the Bronx, Bernard Schwartz. I'm from Philadelphia, myself, originally. I saw *The Passenger* at Cinema Nineteen. The old memories outlive the new ones, Nineteenth Street and Chestnut. There was a huge fat man in the lobby, the 1.10 show, wearing shoes with the toecaps cut away and no socks. I don't think people looked at his toes. Nobody wanted to do that. Then I came to New York and the lampshade in my room started burning. Out of nowhere, flames. I have no idea how I put out the fire. Did I throw a wet towel over the burning shade? I have no idea. Sleep and memory, these things are intertwined. But what I started to say at the beginning, the Japanese movie, I went into the men's room when it was over and the faucets didn't work. There was no water to wash my hands. That's what got me started on this whole subject. The faucets in that men's room and the faucets in this men's room. But there it made sense, there it was unreal like everything else. No people, empty refreshment stand, perfectly clean toilet, no running water. So I came in here, to wash my hands,' he said.

The door behind him opened. He didn't turn to see who it was. Someone standing there, watching, witness to whatever it was that was happening here. A man in the women's toilet, that's all the witness needed to see, a man standing near the row of washbasins, a woman against the far wall. Was the man threatening the woman against the wall? Did the man intend to approach the woman and press her to the hard tile surface, in the glaring light? The witness would also be a woman, he thought. No need to turn and look. *What would the man do to them, Witness and Starveling?* This was not a thought but a blur of mingled images, but it was also a thought, and he nearly closed his eyes to see it more clearly.

Then she was away from the wall. She took two tentative steps toward him, snatched her shoulder bag from the floor and edged quickly along the stalls and past him, around him. They were gone, both women, with Leo feeling he had a desperate second left before he went to his knees, hands to chest, everything from everywhere, a billion living minutes, all converging at this still point.

But he remained where he was, standing. He turned toward the washbasin and stared into it for a time. He ran the water and tapped the soap dispenser, washing his hands thoroughly and methodically, as if to comply with regulations. He paused again, remembering what came next, and then reached for a paper towel, and another, and one more.

The corridor was empty. There were people coming up on the escalator, a late feature about to start. He stood and watched them, trying to decide whether to stay or go.

He came in rain-soaked, climbing the stairs slowly. One step from the third landing he recalled the matching moment of the previous night, seeing himself take the step, one day's end collapsing into the other.

He entered the flat quietly and sat on the cot unlacing his shoes. Then he looked up, shoes still on, thinking something was not right. The pale fluorescent light over the kitchen sink was on, flickering, always, and he saw a shape against the far window, someone, Flory, standing motionless. He began to speak, then stopped. She wore tights and a tank top and stood with legs together, arms raised over her head, straight up, hands clasped, palms upward. He wasn't sure whether she was looking at him. If she was looking at him, he wasn't sure whether she saw him.

He didn't move a muscle, just sat and watched. It seemed the simplest thing, a person standing in a room, a matter of stillness and balance. But as time passed the position she held began to assume a meaning, even a history, although not one he could interpret. Bare feet together, legs lightly touching at knees and thighs, the raised arms permitting a fraction of an inch of open space on either side of her head. The way the hands were entwined, the stretched body, a symmetry, a discipline that made him believe he was seeing something in her that he'd never recognized, a truth or depth that showed him who she was. He lost all sense of time, determined to remain dead still for as long as she did, watching steadily, breathing evenly, never lapsing.

If he blinked an eye, she would disappear. ■

THE MISSION

Tom Bamforth

Food

- Millet / sorghum
  - since farm conflict /
    farming

  - food supplies from
    fast? UNWA

  - income : animal fodder

before conflict

  - lost commerce / trains?
  - animals ufter
  - animals on forrest.

- GS military stayed for 1 year
  - lost battle for Abu Gamra
    August 2004

- Overall fin: insufficient food in
    camps

  - no space for animals in camps
    - families separated
    - animals went over to chadian

It is strange, the rituals we find ourselves carrying out before the unknown – detached acts, learned by rote and made solemn by the occasion. I shaved not once but three times, showered twice, arranged my books first by content, then by colour, then by size. I put on the cleanest of clean clothes – a red shirt, blue trousers, grey desert boots – and stepped out of my dark concrete room onto the street and into the dust of El Fasher.

Outside our compound, as we made final preparations for the mission, there was silent activity, conversation pared back to what was strictly necessary – all the more lucid and eloquent for its truncated, list-like form: ballistics blanket, full medical kit, small medical kit, run bag, 180 litres of petrol, camp beds, water, food, fire extinguishers, satphone, HF radio, VHF radio, radio call-sign list, travel authorization, GPS, white-and-blue flags. Body bags were stored under the back seat of the Toyota Land Cruiser 'Troop Carrier' – a large and highly prized car known throughout Darfur for its speed, agility and long desert range. A car used by aid workers and coveted by killers. Take off the roof, attach a machine gun and you have a 'technical' – a makeshift instrument of war capable of striking deep into the continent. We called it the 'Buffalo' and with its dual fuel tanks, power and relatively light weight, it could cover a thousand kilometres without refuelling. With this car, the chance of attack and hijacking increased, and we had four of them and one hundred kilometres of sand, scrub and stone before us – a lawless area of Sudan known as the Janjaweed Damra. The instructions were simple in this flat no-man's-land whose aridity was starkly etched in dried-up water courses and burned-out villages. Drive as fast as you can.

That, and our rituals. All glowed and squeaked with cleanliness. Beards were neatly trimmed, white robes shone against the sand and sky, the cars were freshly polished and light blue flags of the United Nations flew high. The Muslims among us each had bound tightly around his arm Koranic inscriptions impressed on leather pouches. *Allah, the merciful, the compassionate – keep away the bullets.*

The night before, in a small coffee shop, we had made our final preparations. Everything had been done, the cars stocked and fuelled, fuel dumps prearranged. We had hundreds of forms – forms for assessment, forms for recording, forms for observing. All the bureaucracy for inscribing the needs and living conditions of people living in fear, scared of attack, on the move. Administration for the displaced. I thought I had trained for this, 'skilled-up', prepared. Before moving to Sudan, I had spent two years living and working on humanitarian operations in Pakistan. There I had seen earthquakes that reduced living cities to knee-high rubble; frontier lands where peasant farmers in mud-brick villages were attacked by soldiers of the state, their lands laid waste. Darfur was really where we are needed, I had been told. For the historically minded of our generation the war in Darfur had taken on a moral dimension – this was our responsibility, our Spain. And so we sat finally in the coffee hut – the mission's ten Sudanese members, a Somali security adviser, and I – and in our final preparation raised the questions only our rituals could answer.

For three weeks before the mission in early 2007 – at the same time as the first International Criminal Court indictments for war crimes and crimes against humanity in Darfur – I had listened to the sounds of war, while closed up in concrete offices, protected by scrolls of barbed wire and floodlights and the flags, colours and protective heraldry of the international community. Curfew at seven, radio check at ten: *This is Foxtrot Mike loud and clear.* At six each evening, as I finished work at the office, all thoughts and conversations were drowned by the raw noise and aggression of a Soviet-era Antonov cargo plane taking off on the evening bombing run – the vast hold (meant for tanks) loosely stuffed with bombs which were rolled out by hand into the night.

During the day, I inhabited a small, hot concrete bunker with blocked-in windows. From this makeshift office, I worked as a 'protection officer' trying to gather information about population movements and the humanitarian conditions of people displaced by the Darfur conflict. Going home one evening through a backstreet near the market, I turned suddenly onto the main road and pulled up sharply as a technical accelerated past. Camouflage, rocket launchers, guns and the shouts of men moving out of town, seeking a kill. A roar of noise went up – a full-blooded bark simultaneously bursting from twenty men on edge – as the mounted machine gun slowly turned towards the car. And in the car's cabin, paralysis took hold and my brain went numb, my white and useless strapped-in limbs drooped heavily into the seat. A distended voice – my own – wrenched in through the din with instructions for every muscle and every action. Move slowly, put your hand on the gears, put the car in reverse, move slowly, drive back, go slow, get back, shrink away, retreat. And as they receded, the sweat came, the shaking and the nausea.

At dusk, the firing started from outside town. In our compound, recently equipped with satellite TV, men watched Milan Fashion Week to the irregular detonations from the firing range until it was time for the insurgency channel – amateur videos of militia violence filmed in Iraq, watched by aid workers in Darfur. Parallel realities that only intersected on one occasion when a stray bullet that had been fired into the air smashed through the roof and embedded itself in the concrete floor of the TV room.

Despite the sounds around us, Darfur was remote. Locked away in offices and compounds, barely allowed out because of the passing traffic of militia and the endless fluctuations of alliances between local commanders and factions, Sudan rarely imposed. The billowing dust from a sweeper's broom in the morning, the rich Arabic coffee in the afternoon, took me temporarily away from maps, computer screens, reports of fighting, casualties, people on the move. *They're trying to fuck us over,* my boss used to say each morning, but she was referring to our colleagues in Khartoum.

And so that morning we started, a convoy of white and blue weaving like tracers through the desert. We maintained a tight line of sight and constant radio contact, fanning out to avoid the blinding dust of the car in front. There was strict protocol where the most important positions were the lead and tail, in a defensive formation to protect the cars inbetween. Together, in convoy, watching. We communicated in terse radio form, constantly checking and rechecking our positions. *Mobile Four, Mobile One – are you with us? Over.* Behind us came the vehicle belonging to a lone NGO – outside the UN security arrangements, behind the convoy. Before we left I had gone for a final security briefing. They go for the last car, I had been told. If anything happens, don't stop. They're nice guys, but they're not your responsibility.

But they were – the colour of our flags conferred status, an implication of government, a suggestion of international authority. In the lead car, my white skin had ceased to be my own and, like the flags above, had been lent to the mission as a guarantee of safety.

I was in the lead and yet was the least knowledgeable about this land. I had flown over it before in a small twelve-seater Cessna with a South African pilot offering 'views of Sudan' as the in-flight entertainment. It seemed to me then a landscape of unparalleled bleakness. Sudan was a murderous counterpoint to Pakistan's mountainous north with its soft colours and streams, its hamlets securely tucked away in the mountains. In this desert, I could not survive. I could not read the land or determine a path. My electronic compass simply showed empty space intersected a thousand kilometres to the north by a straight line and the word Libya. My notebooks were a list of twelve-digit map coordinates, measuring degrees, feet and inches east and north, no names or places. Before I left I had seen a political map of Darfur – amorphous colours shifting and blending into one another as alliances broke down, opposition movements split and government favourites charted their own course. The open skies and desert space were strangely and intensely claustrophobic and as we drove my eyes strained, searching the country for checkpoints and militia factions.

And soon enough, we saw the checkpoint – in the distance a little nest of rocket launchers poked over half a dozen sandbags in the sun. I had not seen it, there were no markings, but it commanded the track and marked a random pocket of political control in the sand. Black soldiers from the south, bought and brought by Khartoum, armed by Russia, funded by Chinese oil investments to man an outpost in Darfur. Soldiers of the Government of Sudan.

At speed we continued, and amid the churning dust we passed deserted hut after deserted hut: the remains of villages left gradually to collapse. I saw the black, charred outline of houses burned indelibly into the ground. I shouted at the driver after some subterranean feud over precedence had caused him to clip the tail of the car in front. The surrounding desolation slowly ate its way into our small party. Here, I was told, was the school for boys – a roofless, bullet-ridden building of handmade brick. There was the girls' school – an inferior wooden structure marked by nothing now except a few small pieces of charcoal.

In the storm that engulfed us and stung our eyes and choked us, we walked through an abandoned town where shot-up schools, abandoned shops and bombed wells loomed out of the grey, stinging particles. Near the border of Chad, a child came up to me with his hands on his head and said the single word '*malade*' before disappearing again into the dust.

Animals gathered round a water hole – camels and goats, tended by women in vibrant reds and yellows to the sound of a constant grind and hammer of a water pump. Near our car a man, slightly older than the rest, laughed insanely and struck poses with a Kalashnikov and a makeshift wooden cross-brace, egged on by the men in search of entertainment after a long drive. Eyes wide, hair in matted dreadlocks, grinning, aiming, firing – the sound of imitation gunshots rasping from his distended throat. I took away the cameras and dispersed the teams to get them away from this pitiful, derelict sight. Impassively, our rebel escort looked on from their battered, camouflage technical – the turbaned commander the only adult among them, apart from the driver. A fourteen-year-old stood listlessly holding a rocket launcher and watched with expressionless eyes as the old man refought a war with imaginary weapons and an invisible enemy in front of him.

I walked away from the cars and away from the water hole – the dinning of the pump slowly fading away, the small huts becoming swallowed up in the dust and the uniformly dun-coloured horizon. And on I walked, striding now to get away from the others, almost at a run, so good to use my limbs again after being in the car, away from engines, the crackle of radio contact, the bucking and lurching of the Buffalo as it careened over ruts and ridges in the sand. Behind me was the escort commander, unarmed this time, barefoot in camouflage uniform, and the village elders in white gowns and turbans carrying the walking sticks that marked their high office. On we walked, fast, deliberate, purposeful, away from the village to the forest where the people now lived.

Once again I walked out in front, absorbed in walking, swinging limbs, clearing my head from the perpetual din and fear. I felt relieved to be outside, away from the others, on my own, moving faster and keeping a slight distance in front of the elders and the commander. A sense of purpose had returned after the jarring chase of the cars. But I missed what we were there to see. At a sharp call from behind me, I turned into a thinly shaded wood and saw for the first time houses buried deep inside – camouflaged, all but invisible.

Here was a scene almost of normality – children played under the watchful eyes of their mothers, preparations were beginning for evening meals, fires stoked, wood collected. There were no men – they were away, fighting, moving in a perpetual arc from refugee camps where they were registered and could collect food and organize themselves politically, to their farmland, which they sought to defend, and to their families hiding in the forest. The houses were made of interlaced branches and thatched roofs built around the base of a tree trunk – barely visible from the ground and completely hidden from the air. *We came here because of the Antonov,* they said. *Here we are safe, they cannot see us in the forest.* They had been driven there a year ago; the Antonov had bombed the town and a subsequent land assault by government-sponsored militia had pushed them back, the rebels fighting for the land. Periodically the Antonov returned but there had not been any further land attacks. The defence had not saved the houses but had saved most of the people – already cowering from the air raid, they heard the land attack revving before dawn. *I am just a farmer,* a man told me and reached down quickly, hands trembling, for a cigarette.

And they were not alone. In town after town the same stories of displacement and dislocation were repeated. The mere sound of the Antonov was enough to send people fleeing for the woods and the wadis.[1] Sometimes it just flew over, sometimes bombs would fall, sometimes it was the fatal foreplay to a dawn assault of technicals.

---

[1] Seasonal rivers

Outside another village, I came across a small group of men sitting under a tree. There were about twenty of them and the silence was uncanny. No, they were not from the local village, but they had taken refuge there – under the tree – and had brought some of their animals following a surprise attack only two days before. In the insane calculus of desperation and destruction some of the men had fled quickly, taking as many animals as they could – the income and livelihood of the tribe. They had left women, children and the elderly to find sanctuary in the care of other members of the tribe. But now, having escaped, they feared the worst – that those left behind had been caught in the suddenness of the attack, butchered and raped. As we talked, the temperature rose and the exhausted listlessness was replaced quickly with increasing anger and agitation as the men began to find voice and rage. They were now sleeping rough on the outskirts of the village and knew nothing of what had happened to their families or where they were but thought that the Janjaweed militia might follow them into Dar Zaghawa, even though they suspected that the majority had been killed in the attacks. One man, tall, dark-skinned and dressed with an extraordinary dignity, came to me with a book. Abdul Aziz Adum Haroon, the village teacher, had written down all the names of the people in the village before the attack and had the foresight to take the book with him as he fled. There were 6,200 names.

M y notes became increasingly cryptic, an 'X' in every village becoming the shorthand for the last attack, while number and downward arrows indicated the levels of population decline. And the survey of living conditions ceased to reflect any individuality of person or location and assumed instead an almost bland sameness that emerged from the shorthand of genocide.

Last X 3 months ago. No food, some berries. Water 6 hrs by donkey. Living in forest, animals stolen. Families separated. Majority killed in X. Currently living in wadi. Water holes

bombed/pumps destroyed. Ongoing JJ[2] attacks. Primary/
Secondary displacement. Pushfactors. Antonov seen yesterday at
4pm – live in constant expectation of attack.

> *Shardaba*
> *Songoli*
> *Gurbuhir*
> *Sonjabak*   *Empty/destroyed*
> *Argao*
> *Urubukir*

And then amid these annotations of war, the conflict shone through. They attacked us because of our 'black faces', one man from the town of Doruk told me. And in handwriting shaky from the road, smudged with dust and sweat, a grim record of people's marginal survival was scratched into the page.

GoS[3] harassment – women at risk when collecting water.
7 women from this village have disappeared. Access to water 6 hrs
by donkey. In nearby Ana Bagi, 4 girls had recently disappeared
because of attacks by the GoS forces.
Orschi – Living in forests on seeds and berries and staple millet
(ground-up berries). They might eat meat every 2–3 months, but
have given us one of their goats for dinner.
Hilalia – The Antonov attacked one week ago, and people are
now living in the forest. They had been in camps in Chad but
were also attacked here on a weekly basis by Chadian rebels and
the camp itself was located in an unstable area with little water.
They are safer here than in the camp although things are clearly
difficult. The water well was bombed and daily water collection
takes 5 hrs by donkey – a task that is done by the women. The

---

[2] Janjaweed

[3] GoS – Government of Sudan

SLA⁴ control the area so, currently, this is relatively safe. But –
there is a nearby GoS position and one week ago a village woman
was kidnapped and raped. There was SLA 'retribution' and 'an
exchange' between GoS and the SLA at the water point. The wells,
however, are only full during the rainy season and dry up during
the summer. Food is also scarce and the villagers are dependent
on food from camps in Chad where some are still registered or
through extended family/tribal connections – 5 days away by
donkey. Food collection is also a women's task.

And in this atmosphere of fetid hopelessness we worked. As we talked, stories began to emerge. We came with nothing but our forms to guide us in the recording of conditions in which they lived, and told them that we could not deliver or promise anything. We needed information – who, where and what. But nobody seemed to mind, in many ways it mattered simply that we were there – a presence from the outside, a sign of interest and concern, however small and insignificant. For many, simply telling their story was important in itself. Some people told us about their daily routines – the quests for water, food, the bitter taste of ground berries. On more than one occasion I was taken aside and shown the scars of previous attacks – bullet markings, knife cuts. 'This is what they did – and this.' But always there was the deafening silence of the dead – the subtext of every conversation, the unstated absence in every village – stories present but untold. The only real grief I saw was for a survivor – an elderly man, largely blind and physically weak, saying farewell to his daughters who had made the decision to send him to a refugee camp, where he might have some hope of food and care. In that village near the Chad border, they could barely feed themselves, let alone those who had become dependent. Darfur is not a place where people grow old. The children here had discoloured hair, enlarged stomachs and

---

⁴ Sudanese Liberation Army (a Darfuri rebel group at war with the Khartoum government)

were strangely passive – not moving as the flies settled in numbers around their eyes. Some had decided to move to the camp, others made the calculation that they would risk staying behind – perhaps to be closer to land, farms or family. To all of us watching, it was obvious that, alone and old, the man would not last long and I stood aside, held our convoy, and waited for this last horrendous farewell.

But there were moments of magic, too. I laid out a reed mat on the ground and slept outside each evening and one night, unable to sleep, I climbed over a pile of protective sandbags that were our nominal defences and took the most miraculous night-time stroll of my life, following a moonlit path across a wadi and into Chad. It is the night sky I remember most. I had first become captivated by this in Pakistan where, when work finally finished for the night, I would go outside into the winter cold and look up to see the small rust-coloured dot of a far-distant Mars – fittingly alien amid the profound disturbance of the earthquake zone where I was working. Similarly, in Darfur's desert – seen from space, nothing more than a vast tract of darkness – it became possible to look forward to the pyrotechnic brilliance of the night sky. At a certain point after dinner, conversation would stop and people would lie on the ground gazing upwards, transported away from the sun, the heat and political realities of the day.

We were generally well looked after by the SLA. They accompanied us on all the roads with their battered technicals and teenage soldiers. They dressed themselves in camouflage turbans with arms tightly bound with numerous hijab – small leather pouches containing Koranic verses. Rocket-propelled grenades were strapped to the sides and bonnet of the cars.

The African Union also had a small presence where we stayed in the deserted town called Um Baru. Here, French-speaking Senegalese troops were commanded by a fat Libyan with a large lapel badge showing Colonel Gaddafi waving to a crowd (it was rumoured that if you turned the badge upside down you would get a hologram of Hawaiian dancing girls). However, while the colonel and our SLA escort sipped tea and chatted cordially, this relationship was deeply strained. Only a week before, the SLA had attacked the AU and killed five Senegalese soldiers. Now they were blocking AU access to the water hole in murderous protest against the ineffectiveness of this force in stopping the war.

Fearing attacks on the AU compound, we stayed instead with the SLA, who provided us with a 'guest house', a term that proved somewhat misleading. There was a small concrete bunker with disturbing graffiti scratched into the walls by deranged SLA soldiers. It showed technicals and roughly drawn human outlines shooting fireballs at each other. The other facility was a slaughter area that featured a small tree where each day an apprehensive-looking goat (that evening's meal) would be tethered among the carcasses of its caprine cousins.

Out of SLA territory, however, we had less luck. Our car had broken down and the driver decided to embark on amateur mechanics. This turned into brake surgery and he eventually discovered that he could not get the dismantled parts back together. After five hours of his banging and cursing, we realized that we could not make it through the next GoS checkpoint and into the nearest town before nightfall. The checkpoints are nothing more than soldiers stationed defensively behind rocks or on top of a hill commanding the road. These are sensitive areas and have to be approached carefully – despite wearing GoS uniforms, the soldiers are undisciplined. They resemble a militia more than a regular army and are often hard to see. After dark, they had orders to shoot on sight. We managed to tow the car back ten kilometres to the previous checkpoint and spoke to the commander, who reluctantly allowed us to camp in a wadi under the GoS command post on a neighbouring hill. It was an uneasy night – we encircled our four cars (one with a defunct back wheel, another with a severely bent front axle) and could not light a fire, cook or turn on our torches for fear of being shot at. The sand was soft and warm and the night sky brilliant, but at the change of the guard the new commander took a dislike to us and at 5 a.m. sent a dozen men armed with rocket launchers to move us on.

The strain of the previous night then began to turn into farce. We managed to get our car to the next checkpoint (breaking two steel tow ropes) and rather uneasily left it there, all fourteen people and one sheep piling into the two remaining operational vehicles and limping along as fast as the bent axle would take us. After several overcrowded and dehydrated hours we reached Kutum – the nearest big town with international agencies and the possibility of food and showers. We made our way to the World Food Program, where, despite no food or sleep for two days, we tried to find a mechanic to go back through the Damra with us and claim our car before it was annexed by one of the militias. Standing around making calls on satellite phones, unshaven and unwashed, we suddenly found ourselves in the middle of a delegation that included the newly appointed global head of the World Food Program. In fact, we were so well placed that we formed a grotty and accidental greeting committee: shaking hands, smiling, welcoming the dignitaries to the compound in front of innumerable cameramen, coiffed PR officers and other equally pomaded lackeys rounded up for the occasion. After three arduous weeks in the desert, a passing witness to the imbecility and human cost of war, I stood for a moment in front of one of the most influential humanitarians in the world.

Where's my yogurt, she said . . . ∎

GRANTA

More than thirty years of the best new writing

ISSUE NO 1

ISSUE NO 4

ISSUE NO 6

ISSUE NO 7

ISSUE NO 8

ISSUE NO 10

ISSUE NO 17

ISSUE NO 22

ISSUE NO 67

ISSUE NO 97

ISSUE NO 102

ISSUE NO 108

ISSUE NO 110

ISSUE NO 111

ISSUE NO 112

ISSUE NO 113

ISSUE NO 114

Granta has been home to the most significant writers of our time. We introduced the world to Dirty Realism, redefined travel writing and reported on the fall of the Berlin Wall (30: New Europe!) and the rise of psychoanalysis (71: Shrinks). In the Best of Young Novelists issues (7, 43, 54, 81, 97, 113), Granta was among the first to publish Julian Barnes, Edwidge Danticat, Kazuo Ishiguro, Salman Rushdie, Santiago Roncagliolo, David Mitchell, Lorrie Moore, Jeanette Winterson and many more.

Rediscover literary history.
At granta.com/backissues, every issue of Granta is available to buy –
STARTING AT £7.70

GRANTA

SHE MURDERED MORTAL HE

Sarah Hall

When the fight was over she left the salon tent and walked towards the beach. The way through the jungle was signposted. It was not yet dark. She was not sure what to do. Everything was out of control. She wanted to think clearly, get her bearings. She wanted not to feel so lost, or to feel so lost that nothing more could be taken. Mostly she just wanted to leave their room. She followed the path through the bowed and necking trees. The air was heavy, greenly perfumed, and the avian calls were loud and greasy. The dust felt cool against her feet. She turned left, then right. The path wove through the brush. She stooped under low branches, careful, despite the surging recklessness, where she trod, not wanting to disturb snakes coiled under the leaves.

What's wrong, she had asked him, stroking his back as they lay on the bed after their trip into town. You seem distracted.

Nothing, he had said a few times.

But she had persisted. What? What is it?

After a while he had turned.

Something feels different, he had said. Don't you think so?

They had been together a year. He had said nothing like this before. She had knelt at the corner of the bed and put her arms round herself. He had begun breathing hard, blowing out, as if what he was saying, or was about to say, was heavy labour.

Something feels wrong between us. We should talk about it.

Then, with such terrible ease, it had all begun to unravel. Their meeting at the Halloween party, and his ridiculous bloody stump. Their conversation about Flaubert, the shared cigarette. The kiss, in his terrible heatless flat. The late-night texts. Their first dinner party with its triumphant co-concocted fish soup. The formative moments, winding away, as if they had never been safe.

She picked her way through the foliage, through muggy, scented chambers. Now the birds around her sounded electrical, like mobile phones. Every time she heard a melodic stammer she thought she would come upon someone talking. But there was no one on the path – the lodge was almost deserted, the other salon tents were empty. And there was no phone signal here. An occasional bar crept up on the display, then disappeared, a faint or false satellite. She stopped. All around were intimately knotted branches. The pulp inside the peeling bark was an extraordinary garish orange. There were leopards in here, they had been told by their driver – elusive, flaxen-eyed creatures that were almost never seen. Or seen too late. They were gradually coming back after years of being hunted. And the thought occurred to her that if one of them were to take her now, powerfully by the neck, and drag her up into the crux of a tree, what then? Nothing then. She began walking again.

The tide was on the way out. She knew this even before coming upon the beach. She could hear its retreat, the sonorous hiss at the back of its throat. They had walked this way earlier, after arriving in the complex, to get to the town a mile up the coast, and they'd been surprised by the sudden vertiginous drop. The jungle ended abruptly and the dunes were incredibly steep. There was no gradation. The dark canopy, with its humidity and silicone music, gave way to a long corrugated ramp, ionic sea wind, vast space – two utterly different realms. The trees finished. The air thinned. She saw the ocean for the second time that day, and drew a breath. How had she forgotten its scale, its grandeur? The water was a literal blue. All blues. For a moment the scene looked like one of the cheap plasticized paintings of the Mediterranean on sale in the harbours of southern Europe. But this was not the Mediterranean. This was a body of water so prodigious it looked almost solid, except for the ragged crests, the series of spraying breakers that came from far out and swept up the shore, driving sand high into the jungle. This ocean generated its own wind. It bellowed. Its inhabitants were huge breaching creatures that were of no consequence. After an aborted attempt earlier that day they had not swum. Even knee-deep the undertow had been too strong, dragging their feet down into trenches, making them flap their arms, squat forward and wade against the pull.

The holiday had been her idea. She had read an article in the travel section of the *Guardian*. The writer had urged people to come before the character of the place changed irreversibly. She'd pitched the idea, of being more intrepid, of a different kind of trip, and after a week or two he'd agreed. They had left the hire car at the South African border and been brought to the tiny, fledgling resort in an old white Land Rover with an insecure driver's door that kept swinging open. The driver's name was Breck. He was from Richards Bay, but had come north because the opportunities for new tourism were exciting. He taught scuba and arranged whale watching during migration season. As he drove down the untarred roads he waved to the women carrying canisters and baskets on their hips and heads, and to the children. There were children everywhere. When they passed a man with no hands sitting on an oil drum he said, Look. Long sleeves, I reckon. He's from Zimbabwe. A few have come here. It used to be the other way round. What do you do? he'd asked them.

I'm a lawyer.

Ah. Right. Clever guy. And you?

I manage a company that arranges ghost tours.

Oh, what, to see ghosts?

Places where people have seen ghosts, in London. There are lots of places.

But not the ghosts? No. That's good. Then they can't ask for their money back.

Not really, no.

Though an American woman had fainted in Whitechapel the previous week and had made an official complaint. She had not realized the tour would include spots where victims of the Ripper had been found, she said. She just wanted to see queens and princes. Breck had worked hard to sell the area to them, playing up the economic recovery, making claims about the restoration of wildlife.

The transit vehicle needed to be booked in advance. The border checkpoint closed at 5 p.m. Though she did not want to stay at the lodge that night, though she could not face seeing him after what had been said, or half said, her window to leave was gone.

She waded down the steep sand bank, leaning back, sinking up to her calves. The beach levelled off and she began to walk towards the headland with the cliff path that could be taken into town. Crabs were working the tideline, scissoring pieces of blue jellyfish, dragging the dissections backwards into their burrows. The sun was setting on the other side of the dunes. She could not see any red display, just a dull luminescence above the treetops. She turned and looked behind. The beach was misty with spray and deserted, a long alluvial corridor. He was not following. He would not follow; she knew that. She had refused to let him comfort her after she'd begun crying. He would adhere to this, even if she did not.

She continued on. She replayed the argument in her head, accurately or inaccurately; it did not matter. By the end of the conversation a reptilian dullness had crept into his eyes. It was as if he was persuading himself of his own point of view, of mutual failure.

I used to think you were strange and amazing, he had said. But I wonder how much we have in common. We seem to want different things. Why are we here?

She had stopped crying now, and did not feel sick with panic any more. She felt tender and very alert, as if having risen from a fever, as if driving a new body. There was the reek of kelp all about. Though she was profoundly alone, she felt self-conscious. Observed. To her left, at the top of the rise, the jungle was greenish brown, oily and complicated, immune to the salt air. It was like a mouth, or many mouths, spitting out the sand that it was relentlessly fed. Now that she was looking up at it, the entity seemed superior to the ocean. The uppermost branches shifted and rustled. Nothing flew above.

Nothing flitted in or out. Everything inside was hidden. What was he doing back in their room, she wondered. Repacking his bag, perhaps? Reading a book? Or maybe he was asleep; oblivious to everything, making use of that shut-off mechanism men could rely upon in such situations.

She walked on. The ocean wind was strong. Grains of sand stung her arms and face. Her dress fluttered. Perhaps he was right. Perhaps they were not in step. Why had she wanted to come here, to a place like this, with its memory of recent troubles? Sub-Saharan gothic, he had joked, a busman's holiday. He had booked two weeks off work, which meant handing an important case over to a colleague. They had flown into Johannesburg, visited a few game parks, photographed giraffe and zebra, then come north. They had arrived at midday and the staff had been friendly. The receptionist had kissed them both three times. They had lain on towels and applied sun lotion, and had eaten lunch in a cafe in town. They had talked about going up to the ruined lighthouse on the highest dune to see the sunset. But the sense of this being a holiday was somehow absent. There were still signs of the war – abandoned farms, ruins. Now, separate from him, any meaningful frame for being here was gone. She was anomic. The sand was difficult to tread. Her ankle kept turning. She began to feel foolish.

After a while she turned and looked behind again. There was a white form a few hundred metres back down the beach, where the path to the lodge began. His white linen shirt. Briefly, a sense of elation possessed her. He was looking for her, which meant he was worried. It meant a reversal, perhaps. Should she wait for him or walk on and let him make up the distance? Should she make it easy? She lingered a moment. No. This was his doing. He had instigated their division. He would have to catch up with her. She turned and walked on, not with haste, but purposefully, her steps widening over the dry reefs, the flats of her sandals slapping the soles of her feet. Crabs scattered towards the water. She went about thirty paces. Then she slowed. Perhaps he would not see her so far away. Her dress was pale;

she might be indistinguishable against the sand. And she did want to be seen, didn't she? She paused, looked behind again. The white shape was in the same position, perhaps a little closer. She squinted. The surf was creating an illusory fog; the light was thickening. It was difficult to gain focus. She bridged her hands over her eyes.

The shape was low to the ground, and was not particularly large, not elongated like a man. It was not him. Her disappointment was simply confirmation. She knew he would not come. Still, she was annoyed to have hoped, to have permitted the minor fantasy. The white object was not large, but it was too big to be a seabird. Something mid-sized, then. It was definitely moving; it had velocity, a gait, but she could not tell in which direction it was heading, towards her or away. She peered along the corridor of sand. Towards her. It was coming towards her. She could make out a rocking motion, forwards and backwards, side to side. A creature loping, or running. A spark of alarm fired across her chest. Suddenly there was no air to breathe, though the beach was a cathedral of air. She stood still, lifted a hand to her mouth. A creature running towards her. A creature running towards her. She couldn't move, couldn't make a clear assessment.

There were many dangers here, all outlined in the literature she had received from her health centre. Since arriving on the continent she had retained a prudent fear of the environment. The disease. The bacteria. The wildlife. Not all of it could be washed away, contained, or immunized against. On the way to one of the game parks they had passed an iron-roofed clinic. Outside there had been a long queue of patients. A white doctor was leaning against the clinic wall taking enormous rushed bites out of a sandwich. On the road to the border the traffic had suddenly stopped. After a minute or two the cars ahead had pulled away and driven on, cautiously. A rhino was on the carriageway. It was grazing unspectacularly on the verge as they crawled past. Its plated torso was earth-coloured. Its eye was a tiny dark recess. Twenty miles later they had passed a woman in the middle of the road, waving her arms up and down. Then they'd seen the body, splayed, folded over itself, made boneless by the impact. A young man, walking to work, perhaps. The debris of his briefcase lay in the oncoming lane. It was everywhere, close to the surface, or rupturing through.

She turned and walked on, quicker than before. She lengthened her stride. Whatever was behind her might simply have strayed onto the beach, and would cut up into the brush again, leaving her alone. If it was following without motive, or through curiosity, she could probably make it to the headland pass before it came too close. Just walk, she thought. Walk. Don't run.

The drifts were hard going. The dry crust seemed to support her whole weight for a moment, then became slack and collapsed and her heels submerged. Sand worked its way between her toes. She walked closer to the shoreline, where the ground was firmer and less abrasive, but still her feet seemed poorly designed for the task. They were narrow, hoof-like. Her shins ached. The glow on the other side of the trees was fading. Soon even the dusk light would be extinguished. There were no long twilights like at home. Here the shift came swiftly. She walked on. The crabs scuttled away as she approached, or circled about her feet, their claws held aloft. She did not want to look behind again. Nor did she want to imagine what was there. The latter option was worse. The dress she was wearing was low-backed. Her flesh felt exposed. She was all meat, all scent. Had whatever it was gained? Had it materialized properly? A thing born from the jungle: acute and mindless in its predation, glistening-jawed. Her nails dug into her palms as she paced. It might be a breath away from her. Or it might be gone. Turn, she thought. Turn now.

She stopped and turned and the white shape was coming faster, on all fours. A clean bolt of panic struck against her sternum. She wheeled round. Not far ahead volcanic cliffs rose and an uneven stage of rocks began. She began to run; heavy, stumbling steps. It would be the only way she could make the headland, so she could clamber up to a higher, safer place. But it was like running in a dream. The turgid ground, the dreadful incapacity. She pulled herself forward.

She fought the sand. Her thighs burned, began to seize. Stop, she thought. You have to stop. Showing fear means accepting you are prey. She stopped. She turned and looked back.

It was a dog. A big white dog was coming after her; paws skimming the sand, head held low. It was tracking her. It was engaged in the act, but not at full speed, not in pursuit. She drew herself in, filled her lungs. OK. A dog. A dog was not the worst possibility, even if wild. She'd had the shots, painfully and expensively, in the upper arm, there was still a hard lump under the surface, as if a coin had been inserted. And she could recall no reports in the news of tourists set upon and killed by dogs; such a thing must be uncommon. It was war or malaria or road accidents that spawned tragedy. Though she could recall now, luridly and out of nowhere, the face of that little girl from the north-east, from Sunderland, who had been mauled by the family bull terrier earlier in the year. She could recall her face and neck in the photographs: a grotesque map of welts, flaps and bruises, crescents of black stitches. Then the later pictures: her skull bone grafted over, her nose rebuilt, less striking, surgical disfigurements.

She put her shoulders back, stood her ground, waited for the thing to catch up. When it was within close range the dog lifted its head and veered to the side, then came into line with her, higher up on the ramp of sand. It stopped. The dog looked down at her. Its eyes were dark, bright. Big paws. It was part Labrador, perhaps, blunt-headed, its fur dirty. There was no collar. Its tongue spooned from its jaw. It looked at her. Its eyes were very, very bright. Under the muddy coat was a distended belly and long black teats. It did not appear emaciated.

She was not usually afraid of dogs. She'd had a dog as a child.

Come here, she said. Come. Come here.

The dog dropped its head and came and stood next to her, its warm body pressing against her leg. She put out a hand and let it sniff between her fingers, then she stroked its head, carefully. The fur was damp and gummy. There were lumps on the ears. A stray. But it had once been tame, and it was still tame. Not wild. Not rabid. Biddable. The relief was like stepping into a warm bath. Her muscles relaxed.

She began crying again, though gently, not as she had after the fight. The dog nudged her hand with its head. She petted the dog with the tips of her fingers, combing the sticky fur. It continued to lean warmly against her leg. After a minute she wiped her eyes and walked on again. The dog held back for a moment, then followed and fell in beside her.

You gave me a scare, she said. Listen, I'm not going to keep you.

She continued down the beach with the dog as her companion. She walked slowly. Now and then the dog brushed past and went ahead, then came back to her side. It chased after crabs, bounding towards them, knocking clods of wet sand up with its paws and snapping at the angry, fencing creatures. Then it came to her side again, as if demonstrating obedience.

You know where you're going? she asked. Well, you seem to.

She watched the dog. It was nice to watch. It moved deliberately, in accordance with its proclivities. It sniffed seaweed and chased crabs. Then it wanted to be at her side. For no real reason its presence made her feel better. At the headland rocks they both paused and then picked their way along the puddled outcrop. There were pools the shape of hexagons, strange geological structures. At the edge of the headland the ocean washed over them. As they began to round the cliff, the jungle disappeared from sight. The dog stepped through the shallower pools. It lapped some of the water.

Hey, don't drink that.

She thought perhaps the dog would not come up the cliff path but as she began the ascent it followed, bounding up off its back legs on to the boulders. It squeezed past her where the path was almost too narrow for them both, then wanted to lead. The dog trotted ahead confidently, piloting. Perhaps it belonged to someone in the town, she thought, and had just ranged out. In places she had to bend and scrape through bushes. She brushed her shoulders down afterwards, shook out her dress. The rock was volcanic, sculpted into minuscule peaks. Not far below the ocean hawked in and out of eroded gullies. With the sun off it, the water was no longer the intense blue, but colourless.

It took five minutes to round the headland, and then the settlement came into view, the green-roofed cabins on stilts, thatched huts, the seafood bar, and the little blue Portuguese church with its naive madonna painted on the gable, her figure and head undulating like an expressionist portrait. There were steps carved into the rocks. She walked down them with the dog and along the bay to the launching stage, past a few fishermen who nodded at her, and when she arrived at the edge of the town she stopped.

OK. Go home, she said to the dog. Go on.

The dog sat and faced her. Its teats hung from its black belly. Its claws were long and curved and the webs between looked sore. It cocked its head and looked as if it did not understand the command, or as if she might issue another, preferable instruction. In the failing light its eyes were huge. She made her tone firmer.

Go home. Go. Home.

She clapped her hands in front of its face. The dog got to its feet but did not move. She turned her back and walked away. She glanced back. The dog was not following. It was standing in the same spot on the beach, its ears knuckled upwards, watching her. She continued to walk. When she looked back properly the dog was trotting down to the edge of the water, chasing crabs again.

She did not really know what she was doing, coming into the town. Acting out of anger, but her anger had ebbed now. Though she knew it was relatively safe – Breck, the driver, had vouched for that – she was nervous. She did not want to go back yet. She could not bear the idea of taking up where they had left off. She could not bear seeing him in an altered state, unmoved by her, his eyes blank. She wanted to sit and have a drink, sit and think. She had to get her mind round the situation, had to assimilate it. She'd probably be able to get a ride back to the lodge complex later; locals seemed amenable to casual work. Or she could walk back along the beach. It would be a clear night by the look of the sky. Let him wonder where she had gone. Let him think about things too, what it was he had said, or tried to say, what it was he might be giving up. He was as trapped here as she was, at least until tomorrow when the Land Rover could be booked. If there was a lover he had not yet admitted to – and she had asked, she had demanded to know – he would not be able to reach her by phone to say, yes, he had begun to break things off. No more than she could reach a friend, or member of her family, to be consoled.

She still did not really understand what was going on. He had said nothing about feeling unhappy previously. Why had she asked him, again and again, what was wrong, instead of taking a nap with him on the bed before dinner? Had her asking created a situation that would not otherwise have existed? If she had not asked him, if she had rested her cheek on his back and her hand on his stomach, and had slept for an hour against his side, would the argument never have taken place? Would they still be together? They had had sex that morning, in a different bed, in a game lodge further south. The sex had been good; he had initiated it, and when she had taken him into her mouth he had said her name with surprise, as if at a loss, as if helpless, and he had been desperate to be inside her and they had both moved well, automatically, uniformly, and when she had come he had too. He had seemed moved, looking down at her. Did he know then that later in the day he would be saying such damaging things?

What about this morning, she had said during the argument. You felt something for me then, didn't you?

Yes, he said, something. But that's unfair. It's different. Sex is not rational.

They had bickered on the drive up, about nothing important, when to make a rest stop, whether to buy more bottled water. They had disagreed about whether tourism was a good or bad thing for countries such as this. But the true argument had seemingly come out of nowhere. As if with her arch invitation to speak his mind, she had conjured from a void the means to destroy everything. As if he had suddenly decided it could end. Like deciding he wanted her phone number. Like deciding to get a spare door key cut for her. How easily inverted the world could be. How dual it was.

She made her way along the dirt road towards the cafe. Lights outside the bars were coming on. The evening was still warm. People were sitting drinking beer on the concrete groyne. Three surfers were loading their boards into rusting pickup trucks. There were locals still trying to sell cashews and carvings. The last of the vendors watched her as she passed by but did not approach. Earlier that day they had made good pitches to them both as they lay on towels reading.

Buy these nuts; they are delicious. Just try one for free and then decide.

Perhaps they could witness the recent distress in her, like looking at a dishevelled tract of land a storm has lately passed through. She walked past the oil drum where the handless man had been sitting. She went into the cafe that they had been in earlier, feeling safer for the vague familiarity. She sat at an empty table and the same waiter approached her, a young man, in his twenties, wearing a yellow-and-green T-shirt.

Hello again.

Hello.

He greeted her pleasantly, but she could see that he was confused. He kept looking at the door. This was not a resort, if it could yet be called a resort – locked in by sand roads, and visited by only a few dozen tourists a week – where a woman would drink alone. She had three hundred rand in the pocket of her dress. She ordered a beer. The waiter nodded and went to the refrigerator and brought one over. He set it down on the table with great care, positioning a glass next to the bottle. She thanked him.

Obrigada.

And to eat?

She shook her head. He nodded and withdrew.

She sipped the beer. She thought about him, and what her life might be like without him. They lived in the same city and saw each other regularly, socialized with each other's friends. Most nights they spent together. They had taken a few trips. This was the most exotic – a twelve-hour flight, prophylaxis and rehydration tablets.

They had been getting along fine, she thought. She tried to find any recent tells. Perhaps he had been moody these past few weeks, a little indifferent, stressed at work. He had been curt with her when she said, again, that she wanted to change jobs, that the tours were not what she really wanted to do. But nothing had seemed worrying. She was thirty-one. The thought of going back out, on dates, to parties and clubs, looking for someone, having to generate that intellectual and sexual optimism, made her feel tired. She remembered their first night together. He had taken her for a walk in the park by his house, and out for dinner. They had undressed in the living room of his cold flat and had moved to the bedroom only when his flatmate's door had opened. They had barely slept. They were astonished by each other. The next day they had eaten a late breakfast, gone to the cinema, and come back to the flat to collect her necklace. They had had sex again, better, quick and inconsiderate, her underwear taken off, her skirt left on, and then she had gone to work. She had felt extreme happiness. There had been nothing to lose.

She finished the beer and ordered another. The waiter's politeness increased as he took her order. She knew she was making him nervous. But she wanted the anaesthesia, the insulation. She wanted to go back and not to care about losing him. Part of her thought she should stay out, stubbornly, sleep on the beach, or try to make other arrangements, but she did not have the resolve. She had been gone a few hours; that was enough. If it was over, it was over. She took a few more sips then pushed the bottle away. She put the rand on the table, and stood and left the bar.

OK, the waiter called after her. OK. OK, now.

She felt soft at the edges as she moved, and lesser. Outside the sky was dark, full of different stars. The world seemed overturned but balanced.

A few men called out to her as she walked back towards the beach, not in a threatening way. She did not understand the language and it did not matter what they said. The worst had already happened tonight. In a way she was immune, even from the chill that was beginning. She walked along the beach. It was easier to walk when she felt soft. She was more flexible, more adaptable. There was a quarter moon, brilliantly cut. She could see the shape of the headland and the pale drape of sand leading up to it. The tide had receded. The waves sounded smaller. The crests looked thinner. She could probably walk around the lower section of the cliff now. Beneath everything disastrous, everything menacing, there was honesty. It was beautiful here. She had known it would be. Perhaps that's why she had wanted to come.

As she was walking something loomed up at her side and pushed against her leg. She flinched and stopped moving, then relaxed.

You again.

She petted the dog's head.

Have you been waiting? Look, you're not mine.

The dog was leaning against her, warmly, familiarly. Its coat in the near darkness seemed cleansed. The dog pressed against her and she put a hand on its back. She had avoided touching it properly before, worried about grime and germs. Now she crouched down and took hold of the dog's ears, then under its jaw, and rubbed.

Is that nice?

There was a fusty smell to the animal. The muzzle was wet and when she lifted it up to look underneath she could see it was dark and shiny.

Hey. What have you had your face in, stupid?

Something viscous and warm. When she took her hands away they were tacky. She knew, before the thought really registered, that it was blood.

Oh no, she said. What have you done? What have you done to yourself?

The dog shook its head. Its jowls slopped about. She wiped her face on her inner arm. Perhaps it had gone off and fought with another dog over some scraps while she was in the bar. Or one of the crabs it had been chasing had pinched it. She took hold of the dog's head again and moved it around to try to find a wound, but it was too dark to see properly. The animal was compliant, twitching a little but not pulling back from her grip. It did not seem to be in pain.

She stood up and walked to the edge of the water. She took off her sandals and stepped in. A wave came and soaked the hem of her dress. She stumbled, widened her stance. She slapped her thighs and tried to get the dog to come into the surf, but the dog stood on the beach, watching her, and then it began to whine. After a few attempts she came back out.

OK, she said. You're fine. Let's go.

They walked towards the headland and when they reached the rocks they stayed low and began to pick their way around the pools and gullies. This time the dog did not pilot. It kept close, nudging against her legs. When she looked down she could make out a dark smear on her dress. Where the outcrop became more uneven she bent and felt her way using her hands and was careful where she put her feet. The largest waves washed over the apron of rock against her shins. Towards the end of the headland, water was breaking against the base of the cliff. She timed her move and went quickly, stepping across the geometric stones. A wave came in and she heard it coming and held tightly to the rock face as it dashed upwards, wetting her dress to the waist. She gasped. Her body was forced against the rock. She felt one of her sandals come off. Water exploded around her and rushed away. The haul of the ocean was so great she was sure she'd be taken. She clung to the cliff. Every atom felt dragged. Then the grip released. She lurched around the pillar onto the flat ground, grazing her ankle as she landed. She winced and flexed her foot. She took off the remaining sandal and held it for a moment. Then she threw it away. She wrung out the bottom of her dress. She looked back. The white dog was standing on the other side of the rocky spur, its head hanging low.

Come on, she called. Come on.

It did not move.

Come on, she said. Come on.

The dog stayed on the rocks for a moment and then turned and she could see it was going back the way they had come.

She watched its white body moving. It floated. There seemed to be nothing holding it up. When the shape disappeared she turned and faced the long steep stretch of beach. The ramp of sand disappeared into the black jungle. The white tideline disappeared into the dark body of the ocean. Only the pale boundary was visible. Tideline meeting sand. She began to walk. She could not remember exactly where the hotel path was, about a mile away, but there was a signpost right by it, she knew that. She walked for a long time, feeling nothing but sand grinding the soles of her feet and chafing her ankles, salt tightening on her skin. She prepared herself. She could accept the end now. She could embrace it. No one was irreplaceable. No one. He could go. She would let him go. She did not like his friends, the smug barristers, the university clique, because they did not like her, because she was not their sort. She did not like his reticence or his conservatism, the way he drove, the way he danced. She would miss the sex, the companionship, until she found someone else. And she would find someone else. Let him join the men of the past. Her old lovers were ghosts. None of them had survived; none were missed.

After a while she stopped. She had come too far. She must have missed the let-out. She doubled back and after a time she saw the small skewed signpost at the top of the dune. She leaned forward and climbed up the bank towards it. Sand spilled backwards, skittering down the slope as she moved. Her legs ached. She felt exhausted. All she wanted to do was lie down and sleep. She sat for a moment at the top of the rise and looked at the ocean – a relentless dark mass. Tomorrow she would probably not see it. Then she stood.

The entrance of the path was nothing but a void in the jungle. There was still some warmth inside the foliage as she entered. She bent over and felt her way along, through the trees, to the wooden steps and up. She trod carefully. Occasionally she stamped a foot and the noise echoed dully. Under her feet the fine drifts of dust were cold. There was no light, no reflection. She felt invisible. She felt absent. She made her way through the trees, holding her hands out before her and feeling for low-hanging branches. Her eyes adjusted but the darkness continually bled back into their sockets and she had to fight blindness. The birds and the insects were silent. Then, the low-wattage lights of the outer salon tents.

Before she reached the complex she heard agitated voices. She could not make out the words. She wondered whether he had raised the alarm. She was embarrassed by the thought; by the idea that people might know she had acted rashly, and why. As she came into the clearing where the main lodge was she could see a group of people standing together. He was not among them. Some of the staff were there, speaking earnestly to each other in Portuguese and an African language. One of them, the woman who had given them their key earlier that day when they checked in, had her arms wrapped around herself and she was rocking slightly. The fuss was embarrassing.

She thought about slipping back to the tent, unseen. She held back for a moment, and then she approached. They turned to look at her. No one spoke. Then the receptionist cried out, came towards her, gripped her painfully by the arms, and looked towards the men.

Ela está aqui! Ela está aqui!

I went for a walk. On the beach.

The woman released her and took a step backwards and raised her hand as if she might be about to strike her. Then she shook her hand and flicked her fingers.

Você não está morta?

I just went for a walk, she said again. What's happening? I'm all right.

There was a period of confusion. The discussion resumed and broke down. The receptionist shook her hands and walked away, into the shadows. She wanted to leave too, go back to the salon tent, face what she must and then sleep, but the intensity of the situation held her. Something was wrong. Her arrival back at the complex had not lessened their distress. One of the men in the group, the sub-manager, stepped forward. He gestured for her to follow. She walked with him to the entrance of the main lodge. By the doorway, on the ground, there was a bundle of cloths. They were knotted and bloodstained. The man pushed them aside with his foot, into the corner of the wooden porch. She began to feel dizzy. Heat bloomed up her neck.

What is it? she asked. Has there been an accident?

OK, he said. OK. Come inside.

He went through the door. She followed him into the bar and the man gestured for her to sit at a stool and she sat. His face was damp. He was scratching his arm. She heard others from the group entering the bar behind them.

Ah, he said. OK. Your husband. He was looking around for you. He went to find you. He was very worried. He was . . . there was an attack, you see.

He was attacked? By who?

No. Not a fight. We don't really know how it happened. He was found by George one hour ago. Outside, in the dunes. But he was not conscious. There was a lot of blood. The wound is . . .

He called over to the group of men by the door.

Ei, como você diz tendão?

Tendon.

Yes. The bite is in the tendon of his leg. It's very deep. And a lot of blood is gone. Breck is taking him to the hospital. They will probably have to go to Maputo in the ambulance.

She brought her hands to her face.

Oh my God, she said. Oh my God. I didn't think he would come after me.

Her palms smelled musty, like old meat, like a sick animal. She took them away from her mouth and looked up at the man. He was watching her, nervously. His eyes kept flicking away and back towards her, as if she might react dangerously, as if she might faint or bolt. She shook her head.

What was it? Was it a leopard?

No, he said. No. No. There are no leopards. ■

GRANTA

A GARDEN OF ILLUMINATING EXISTENCE

Kanitta Meechubot

I

The images in 'A Garden of Illuminating Existence' were inspired by my grandparents' lives and the story of their marriage. I wanted to trace the different branches of my grandparents' – my family's – journey, to find out where they had come from, where they had been. And so I sought out the crumpled leaves of faded photographs and old pictures hidden in dusty boxes in the attic. I found a way of reimagining and commemorating my grandmother's painful final years battling womb cancer.

II

When my grandmother is diagnosed with the disease, Death, a skeleton, entices her to give up hope, to surrender. In these pictures, the dark background is not emptiness but an element itself, highlighting the delicate objects that give her the strength to resist. I imagine her cancer as hellish flames inside her belly. The pain spreads like a great forest fire, just as chemotherapy burns her from the inside. She is trapped, a prisoner in her own body who can only find escape in her retreat to a world of memories.

III

Finally, exhausted, she allowed herself to die. This is the way I want to remember her, the lost one beneath the tree as her body decomposes. Trees link the sky and earth, pointing to the infinite journey on which she is about to embark, the roots of the tree integrating with the human heart, the spine, the muscles and the veins. She will return in another form of life; tree roots will pull her soul above the ground. Then she and my grandfather – Chalaem and Samarn, the lovers – will hold each other again inside the heart of a tree.

IV

I find myself telling and retelling the story of their romance. Their first meeting is like the spring when flowers are reborn and the heavy scent of new blossom permeates the air. In the summer their relationship ripens – they marry, raise a family, retire into old age. In the blustery fall of leaves in autumn her illness is revealed and then, finally, the death-carriage bears her away when winter comes.

They had been married for sixty years. I had never seen him cry until that morning on Valentine's Day in 2006. And even now I can see the sorrow in his eyes as he watched her disappear. He wept as if his bones ached.

But as she passed away, her face looked relaxed and calm, almost as if she was telling him: *It is time for me to go to sleep. There is nothing to cry about. We will see each other soon.*

Witnessing her death, I understand the meaning of love. ■

I.

2.

3.

4.

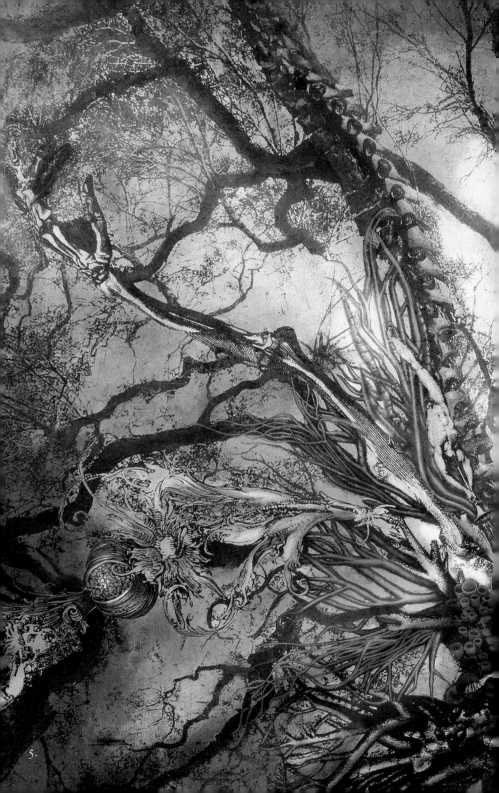

5.

8.

9.

DENG'S DOGS

Santiago Roncagliolo

TRANSLATED FROM THE SPANISH BY ALFRED MAC ADAM

My earliest memory of Peru is a newspaper photograph from 1980 of dead dogs hanging from lamp posts in downtown Lima. Their stiff bodies were wrapped in posters that said: DENG XIAOPING SON OF A BITCH. In the picture, bewildered policemen are cutting down the bodies in the early-morning light. Some of the dogs drip blood, others are painted black, but most are simply dead.

I was living in Mexico, where my family had been granted political asylum. My father was neither a terrorist nor a bomber. He was just a left-wing journalist. But back in those years, that was reason enough to be exiled. We would avidly read any news about Peru, and on this occasion the papers carried a photo of cops cutting down dogs. The street beyond the dogs looked filthy, dismal. To me, the black-and-white photo was the real colour of the city. I was five years old and that, insofar as I understood things, was my country.

In our house, the picture – and the murders that came later – was the subject of lengthy deliberations. My father's friends wondered if the time was ripe for a revolution in Peru. For all of them, revolution in Latin America was imminent, as inevitable as hurricanes in the Caribbean. They never wondered *if* it would come but only *when*, and in which countries it would triumph. At home, in long sessions cloudy with cigarette smoke, bearded men in tortoiseshell glasses would debate, conspire, or just hide out.

While my 'uncles' were changing the world, we, their children, would play in my room. We must have been a rather picturesque gang – preschool kids with Sandinista Front for National Liberation T-shirts and Che Guevara notebooks. Our identification papers all said 'political refugee'. I had a T-shirt with Saddam Hussein's picture on it. My favourite game was 'guerrilla warfare'.

I lived in this alternate reality until the day democracy returned to Peru, and freely elected President Fernando Belaúnde guaranteed all exiles a peaceful return. My parents were happy to return to our country. But I remembered those dogs hanging from lamp posts and didn't think it was such a good idea.

In the mid-1980s, the Shining Path was fast becoming the most lethal guerrilla force on the continent. These revolutionaries looked nothing like my father's friends; in point of fact, they were more radical than most Latin American subversive groups: they considered Cuba a right-wing state; the Soviet Union an imperialist equivalent of the United States. And the 'open' China of Deng Xiaoping was for them a revisionist regime that had betrayed true revolutionary values. They also held Che Guevara, whom they called a 'bourgeois clown', in contempt. And they were right about one thing: Che's military strategy was useless in the nations of the Andes. After all, he had been captured and put to death in Bolivia, a country geographically similar to southern Peru. So rather than copy the tactics of guerrillas all over the continent, the Shining Path studied Mao's experiment and designed a war for poor peasants, or peasants who were in a pitiable state beyond poverty.

Instead of buying weapons from Cuba or Nicaragua, the Peruvian Maoists killed people with rocks, clubs and knives in hand-to-hand combat. That gave them operational independence. But it also desensitized them when it came to using violence. Besides, the *senderistas* wore no uniforms but disguised themselves as civilians and under this cover harassed the army. In turn, the armed forces began firing on the civilian population. Finally, the *senderistas* tried not to win over the population because it was equally effective to terrorize them. For instance, in the early 1980s in the village of Lucanamarca, they used machetes to kill sixty-nine people in a single day. And ten years later, on 16 July 1992, they packed a car with half a ton of plastic explosives and blew up a business street called Tarata during the rush hour. Twenty-six people died that night, with 150 wounded. More than four hundred businesses and 164 apartments were destroyed. Doing things like that made them into the most lethal guerrilla force on the continent.

The Shining Path took control of a third of rural Peru. But to win the war against the state they would have to conquer the capital, which is where I lived. The *senderistas'* strategy was to seize control of the poor neighbourhoods around Lima and from there to attack the population within the city. Tales of hordes of beggars who would some day charge down from the hills to attack our houses and steal our belongings fuelled my childhood nightmares.

The violence also created daily inconveniences. We learned to put tape on our windows so they wouldn't shatter when the shockwave from a bomb blast hit. We learned to dive for the floor when we heard shots. If we ate out, we would dine early so we could get home before curfew or, conversely, we would go to parties very late so we could return after curfew. We learned never to park opposite military installations because the soldiers had standing orders to fire on any parked car. Over time, you can get used to anything.

The most frequent – the signature *senderista* terrorist attacks – were power outages, which they produced by dynamiting the towers carrying high-tension wires. They always chose Christmas or New Year, when families would be at home, to inflict maximum inconvenience. And always at midnight. Power outages were the only events in Peru that took place punctually.

The Shining Path used these outages as a show of strength, and to confirm their message they'd often follow up with explosions in the hills surrounding the city. Another treat were fires in the shape of a hammer and sickle, blazing in the night. No one dared to put them out.

One day in May 1999, almost twenty years after I saw the photo of the dogs, I entered the Picsi jail in the northern city of Chiclayo. It had been designed for 300 prisoners, but at the time it held 974,

252 condemned for 'acts of treason against the Nation', the legal term that included terrorism.

By then the reign of the Shining Path seemed like ancient history. For seven years, we'd had no bombs, no power outages, and the *senderistas* leader Abimael Guzmán was in prison. End of story. Apart from that, I knew very little about the history of the movement, and until then I had never seen a terrorist with my own eyes.

It was the first time I'd ever entered a high-security prison. At the entrance, a policeman took away my camera. And two steps inside, the air seemed twice as heavy as outside. Between the Picsi prisoners and freedom there were two walls, each eight metres high, topped with barbed wire and separated by what was called a no-man's-land, a grey, arid space ten metres wide.

No-man's-land was the first sign we were entering hell. The police playing cards and wiping off the sweat on their necks with their shirtsleeves knew that this was not the best place for getting promoted, and they eventually took out their frustration by spitting on the cell bars. Many of the prisoners leaning against those bars hadn't seen anything but those walls for ten years: their outdoor time was limited to the yards inside each pavilion. For sixteen prisoners with life sentences in Pavilion E, no-man's-land was the last horizon they'd ever see.

In those days, I worked in the Public Defender's Department, a government institution whose remit included supporting the work of the human rights activist Father Hubert Lanssiers. The government's counter-terrorist policies had resulted in the unfair arrest and incarceration of hundreds of innocent men. Lanssiers had been charged by the president with interviewing prisoners who had requested re-evaluation. He would review their cases and recommend pardons if he thought they had been jailed without proof or had been the victims of bogus trials during the last years of the war against terrorism. Lanssiers was not popular with the authorities, and public opinion was also against him. The entire country believed that it was better that ten innocent men be in jail than for one terrorist to be free. After seven years of peace, the army and the police could admit a few mistakes. They would call these abuses 'caring too much' about security.

That day in May 1999, Lanssiers, two lawyers and I walked into Pavilion E. Lanssiers, the tallest, led the way through the phalanx of prisoners, who silently made way for us to pass. I noted nervously that we had no escort, and when we reached the pavilion's central patio, where the tables for ceramic work and the weights with which the prisoners worked out were located, I understood we wouldn't need any.

The imprisoned *senderistas* did not glare at us in the defiant, challenging and proud way they did when posing for the camera crews that recorded their arrests. And they weren't shouting out the incendiary slogans I had seen emblazoned on their banners. Some of them were arrogant, but Lanssiers' stare was even tougher than theirs, and he spoke with a confidence that won respect. 'I've been here for eight years,' said the first prisoner we interviewed. 'And I was sentenced to twenty more. I was locked up because a neighbour who was a terrorist and who wanted to get even with me lodged a false accusation. My family is on the outside – just three women and a boy. They can't farm my land, so we're going to lose it. My daughter became a prostitute just to survive. What's the use of having me here? If my case isn't reviewed soon, what's going to become of my children? Of course they're going to become criminals.'

I whispered to the lawyer who accompanied me: 'This guy was screwed over. He's right.'

The lawyer smiled and whispered in my ear: 'This guy? This is Comrade XXX. He murdered twenty-six people in cold blood. His case has already been reviewed.'

Lanssiers listened to every man who spoke and assured each one that cases would be examined, but that anyone who had committed murder would never be freed. He didn't say it to challenge them. It was, simply, the truth. But he said it looking right at Comrade XXX and other prisoners whose crimes he knew. I was impressed at the respect he showed even them, the murderers, as he fixed his gaze on them. I later discovered that was the same way he looked at the police, government functionaries and lawyers. It was a stony blue-eyed stare that reduced everyone to the same level. You were a human being, nothing more, nothing less.

It was hard for me to understand that stare of his and the fact that he hated no one. Some of the Picsi prisoners had taken part in the Tarata attack, which took place a kilometre away from where I was living. The apartment of a family friend was blown to pieces. It could have been mine. So that day, in Pavilion E, face to face with the perpetrators, I felt absolutely no pity for them and certainly no respect.

We left Picsi when it was already getting dark, worn out after talking with more than a hundred men. We needed a drink. In the hotel bar, Lanssiers ordered a glass of milk and spoke more readily but still in the same direct Spanish he used to speak to the *senderistas*. Only his Rs betrayed his francophone origins. He smoked black-tobacco Incas, the cheapest and smelliest cigarettes on the market. He would light the next with the butt of the one he was finishing. I eventually worked up the courage to make a point: 'You seem very used to talking with murderers.'

'The important thing is that they get used to me,' he answered drily.

'Of course. But it's easy to see that you didn't live through what we did. Since you're a foreigner . . .'

I said that with a certain air of condescension because I was used to well-intentioned Europeans who thought the laws that worked in Sweden would work in Peru. Like many Peruvians, I accepted the ever tougher laws against terrorism and drug dealing, even those allowing terrorists to be judged by anonymous tribunals. That was the way to subdue them.

Other things annoyed me. During those years the Intelligence Service had expanded its powers to the point where it controlled practically everything, and the Internal Revenue Service had become a political blackmail agency. The government had dissolved the Constitutional Court and nullified the jurisdiction of the Inter-

American Human Rights Court. But I still believed – a point I tried to make to Lanssiers – that in order to democratize the regime all subjects related to terrorism had to be removed from public debate, because they only discredited those of us who favoured democracy.

After listening to my argument, which I thought ironclad, Father Lanssiers smiled and ordered another glass of milk. Then he said to me: 'When I was a boy, I lived in a small city near Brussels. I remember the immense joy we all felt on 10 May 1940, when we got to school and found the doors locked. We didn't know why. It's true that war was in the air. Hitler's speeches were on the radio and my parents, who spoke German, knew what was going on. But my friends and I were eleven years old, and all that seemed a bit fanciful to us. So we went home, running around and playing. Five minutes later, planes appeared in the sky, and people came out shouting to us to get down on the ground as the bombs began falling. Playtime was over.'

Lanssiers' voice appeared to have only one tone. At no time did it get louder or express emotion. He could recount an execution as if it were a recipe. This was the case even when he talked about his family. 'My grandmother had it much worse than we did. She lived on the triple border of Holland and Germany, where the Germans launched a parachute attack. The SS invaded the village and shot her. My aunt died buried under the ruins of her own house. The people who found her saw that her death hadn't been instantaneous because on the ground next to her were the marks left by her nails as she tried to scratch her way out. In that town, not a single house was left standing.'

From that moment on, as Father Lanssiers told it, his family lived and slept in the basement, where there was less danger from bombs. When they finally managed to flee towards the sea, the Messerschmidts followed them all along the road to Dunkirk where the British were boarding ships. The one the Lanssiers were to escape on was sunk and amid the terrifying sirens of the bombers, the blown-up tanks and the corpses, Lanssiers remembered his mother gathering her children together so that, at least, they would all die together.

His mother had experience of war. She'd been captured several times by the Germans during the First World War in Liège where she'd served as a courier for Free Holland. His father, moreover, was a rabid socialist who'd fought in the Foreign Legion. At home, the family awakened to the sound of the bugle and went to sleep with the Internationale as a lullaby. I asked Lanssiers if being a socialist wasn't practically a crime to the Nazis. He presented me with a smoky smile: 'It was all the same. The mere fact of existing was a crime to the Nazis.'

When he finished his tale – which utterly demolished my argument that 'he hadn't suffered the way I had' – I fully expected a homily about tolerance and forgiveness. But it never came. Lanssiers didn't pontificate or philosophize about that time beyond a few words charged with black humour. His feelings seemed composed of a sceptical silence. I had to ask: 'Why did you choose to come to Peru?'

Lanssiers swallowed the rest of his milk and stuffed out his cigarette in the overflowing ashtray. 'I haven't been able to choose many things in life.' Then he said goodnight and went up to his room. The next day, we all went back to Lima.

Some weeks after the visit to Picsi, a report reached my office about an incident that had taken place in the Yanamayo Maximum Security Prison in Puno, a place high in the Andes near the border with Bolivia, where several *senderistas* leaders were serving their sentences.

Conditions in Yanamayo had already brought about rioting. The temperature would fall to -10°C at night, and there was no heating. The prison was far from any town or military installation, and the National Police (themselves under military control) rarely allowed personal visits or civilian inspections. This most recent riot had sparked when prison authorities tried to confiscate all radios, which were prohibited inside the jail, along with books, magazines and newspapers. The prisoners refused to hand over their radios. The police called in a regional prosecutor who, following established procedure, made an 'official' demand. Again, the prisoners refused. Without repeating the demand, the prosecutor departed, leaving the prison in the hands of a battalion from the Special Operations Command.

The next day, three terrorist leaders were evacuated. The bruises on their bodies showed they'd been raped with nightsticks, which the authorities referred to as 'the rods of the law'. No other criminals were allowed to leave.

The press did not cover the incident. No one mentioned it. Many newspapers at the time were carrying out a campaign to show that candidates opposed to the government were homosexuals. One of the papers, *El Chino*, had actually published a photo of two pigs' heads. Under the picture were the names of the anti-government candidates.

My office could not release information about Yanamayo without sacrificing the already slight confidence the military had in us, so we had no possibility of intervening. The report had come to me simply so that I could correct the spelling and punctuation. But I wondered how many similar situations were happening out of the public eye. Murders carried out 'for our well-being'. How many crimes were silently allowed to go unprosecuted, because nobody wanted to know?

I started to hear stories. A few months later, during an official trip to the city of Ayacucho, the birthplace of the Shining Path, I was introduced to a peasant, Angélica Mendoza, who led an association of the families of the disappeared. At dawn, on 2 July 1983, the army had taken away Angélica's son, Arquímedes Ascarza. Angélica remembered that there had been about thirty men armed with rifles and automatic weapons, some wearing uniforms, others in civilian clothes. They got out of two trucks and almost knocked the door down as they forced their way into her house. They beat Arquímedes's brothers, kicked his father and threatened them with rifles as they lay face down on the floor. They searched – that is, destroyed – the house, looking for something, although no one knew what. All they found was Arquímedes, barefoot and in pyjamas. Swearing and cursing, they dragged him outside.

Despite the weapons pointed at her face, Angélica clung to Arquímedes with all her might. So they dragged her to the truck too and kicked her until she let him go. Angélica screamed for her neighbour Eutemio, a policeman, to help, but he wouldn't leave his house. From the truck, Arquímedes told his mother to pick him up the next day at the barracks. That was the last time she saw her son. He was nineteen and had dreams of joining the police force.

Hours after her son's arrest, Angélica's tragic odyssey through the barracks and police stations in Huamanga province began. The army said it knew nothing, that maybe the Republican Guard might have information. The Republican Guard sent her to the Civil Guard, who suggested the Investigation Police. Everywhere, the answer was always the same: 'We know nothing, *mamacita*. We know nothing.'

Nothing.

Two weeks later, a man suspected of terrorism but now freed from the Los Cabitos military base, handed Angélica a letter from her son. The writing was shaky, but it at least reassured her that her son was alive. Arquímedes told her he'd been tortured, that if he complained, they'd shut him up and torture him again. His cellmate told Angélica that a woman, unable to endure more torture herself, had denounced Arquímedes as a terrorist. That's why he was imprisoned. The last thing the cellmate had learned was that Arquímedes had been put on a helicopter.

Mad with despair, Angélica began to search the ravines where the bodies of the dead were tossed: Puracuti, Paycochallocc, Huascahura. One constant in the bodies she found were signs of torture. Sometimes, the physical mistreatment was so severe it was the obvious cause of death. Other times, she'd find bodies with their hands tied behind their backs, on their knees, with bullet wounds in the back of the neck or temples. Generally, the executioner delivered the coup de grâce in the back of the head so he wouldn't have to look his victim in the eye.

The technique for effacing the identity of the bodies varied. Many were blown apart with explosives or had their eyes gouged out.

Soldiers often guarded the mass graves. Sometimes, Angélica tried to dig up the graves, and soldiers would threaten to kill her. Her only response was, 'If you want to kill me, kill me, but first tell me where my son is.' The nervous soldiers would insult her, shove her, pull her away from the ravines, but she'd insult them in turn and fight over the bodies with the scavenging dogs and pigs that inevitably gathered at the mass graves. All she wanted to know was if Arquímedes was there, the only thing she needed was confirmation of his death.

None of the young conscripts had the nerve to shoot at her. As they became ever more familiar with her, they stopped trying to keep her out. On one occasion, in the Quinua cemetery, not far from Ayacucho, the police even disinterred fifteen bodies so that Angélica could look them over. 'None of these can be your son,' they said. 'These were brought by navy people at Esccana.' Angélica recognized a teacher from San Miguel and his entire class. Before she left, the police said to her, 'You are a mother, we all have mothers. Pray for us, please, so that nothing happens to us.'

Other times, she would get to a mass grave only to find that the bodies had no heads or that the faces had been painted over. As Angélica told me her story, I began to think that we were from two different countries at war with each other. In mine, all I had to do to protect myself was to put tape on my windows to keep them from breaking. Angélica could do nothing.

Lanssiers would frequently visit my office – actually the office of my boss, the Public Defender. Whenever he came, I tried to chat with him, but he didn't remember me or our conversation. And even if he did, he was not the kind of person who wasted time in idle chit-chat. He went straight to business.

At one point Lanssiers published a collection of articles and my boss offered either (I don't remember which) to host a presentation or to write something about the book in the newspaper. Politicians have no time to write and part of my job was to write the speeches and articles that my boss then revised and signed. The article on

Lanssiers' book was no exception.

The collection consisted of old articles about emergency humanitarian situations the priest had witnessed in Asia. His style was as acrid and cutting as his manner of speech, and his common-sense attitude neutralized the brutality of the events he described.

I isolated the facts of Lanssiers' biography so I could write my review. After the Second World War, Lanssiers joined the Allied occupation army in Cologne. His comrades sold weapons, blew up houses using compressed air bombs, exchanged cigarettes for women. Nevertheless, they still seemed more civilized than the Nazis. Later, in the mid-1950s, he joined the Congregation of the Sacred Hearts of Jesus and Mary and went off to do missionary work in Hokkaido, the coldest, most miserable and most solitary part of Japan. Finally, he was sent to Indochina, at the same moment the Khmer Rouge was on the rise.

His job was giving spiritual support to Catholics wherever he could find them. There were not many. No less important was the information he sent to his superiors in Japan.

As a 'spy for God', Lanssiers tried to get into Saigon before the Vietnamese took control, but he arrived three days too late and had to flee to Cambodia with the French forces who had fought against the Communists and were now retreating towards the Mekong. For a decade, he lived through the French withdrawal, the arrival of the Americans, and the advance of the Vietcong (on one side) and the advance of Pol Pot (on the other). He travelled with the South Vietnamese rangers who invaded Cambodia. Fascinated by the war, Lanssiers felt right at home with the combatants. 'Even the stomach problems I'd had for a long time disappeared as soon as I arrived.' Instead of battle fatigue, he felt frustration when he learned of a fight in which he couldn't participate.

But the major conflicts did end, as did his adventure. In 1979, his superiors in Japan ordered his transfer, and he found himself aboard a banana ship sailing from Tokyo to Latin America. By then Lanssiers looked more like an adventurer or a refugee than a priest.

At this point in my life, I was fed up with Peru. Before I worked in the Public Defender's Office, I was a scriptwriter for a TV soap opera. The channel, which also had an opposition news programme, was expropriated from its owner by the government, and turned over to the minority shareholders. The programming changed. My next writing opportunity was scuppered when the principal actor in the comedy I was to write scripts for was hired away by the state channel, and his writers were assigned by the junta. Television work disappeared from my future.

Later on, an official newspaper hired me as a journalist. It was almost a fictitious business, because it was never really sold on the streets. Its only function was to publish front pages favourable to the government. In turn, the government showed its thanks by supporting the owner's other businesses. Many of the political columnists didn't believe in what they were writing but they had families to support and so they didn't complain. The editorial writers created a contest – who could write an article in favour of the government in the shortest time? The record was five minutes twenty seconds.

My prospects, you see, were pathetic. Even so, compared with the stories I kept discovering about people like Angélica Mendoza, my problems seemed more like those of a spoiled rich boy. I suppose those of us who've had a religious education but whose families are left-wing have two handicaps: guilt and that thing we call a 'social conscience'. We may try to repress them, but it's impossible. I felt like a bourgeois cockroach.

So I embarked on a modest heroic quest of my own. I decided to immerse myself in the subject of the disappeared in order to write an article that would include statements by Lanssiers. I hoped his name would enable me to sell the piece to one of the opposition newspapers. After all, Lanssiers had been linked to the paradoxical combination of humanitarianism and terrorism ever since those issues had taken centre stage in Peru. But he avoided interviews, political statements, or taking a position. That attitude enhanced his value.

I thought, given what I knew about him, that I could get Lanssiers to make some forceful comments. With regard to general information about the disappeared in Peru, I had at my disposal the institution where I worked and its archives. The Public Defender's Department analysed 7,762 disappearances, of which 1,674 were found alive, 514 were found dead, and 4,022 remained in a mysterious limbo. Years later, we would learn that almost 70,000 people had died or disappeared since 1980, more than those who had disappeared as a result of the repressions of the Chilean and Argentine dictatorships combined.

I thought all that information would oblige the taciturn Lanssiers to make a forceful statement. Besides, a new factor was nourishing my hopes: at the time, the commission in charge of pardons for the innocent had finished its work. The Public Defender's Department had announced its decision to place observers in the 2000 elections. To punish us, the government transferred all the commission's pending cases to the Justice Department. It was a favourable moment for Lanssiers to raise his voice against the regime.

I spent two weeks annoying his secretary before getting through to him. I told her that I had to speak with him in person without admitting that what I wanted was an interview – a request I suspected he would probably turn down. Every time I called, I repeated that I was working in the Public Defender's Office, in the hope of gaining her confidence. Finally, I did get to speak with the priest, and I requested the interview. 'Are we going to talk about politics?' he asked. 'I don't talk about politics. There are things that are not worth discussing.'

'We're going to talk about your memories, Father Lanssiers. Your story.'

'Frankly, I have no idea who'd be interested in my story.'

But he did grant me the interview, even though he still did not remember me.

L anssiers received me in an austere office inside a school attended by middle-class boys and girls and run by his order. From the moment he lit his first Inca, we both understood that we were engaged in a fight. I wanted him to give me a juicy headline, and he wanted to stick to his story about working in the prisons.

'The first time I walked into a pavilion crowded with *senderistas* in the Frontón prison, I was given an icy reception,' Lanssiers told me. 'When I asked to speak with their delegate, I was sent from one man to another, until I said, "This is like the Vatican when you want to talk to the Pope. First you have to talk to the bishop and then with another bishop who takes you to a monsignor, who takes you to another . . ." But my comment had no effect. They had no sense of humour. When I finally managed to meet the delegate, he tried to indoctrinate me. I had to make a deal: "I won't catechize you, and you shouldn't catechize me." Then we began to get along well.'

In the eighties, the *senderistas* were not like the other prisoners. They believed they belonged to an unbreakable collectivity. They had their own ceremonies with red banners and pictures of Mao. They wore khaki uniforms in the Chinese style and marched singing anthems, all with much more discipline than the police. Paradoxically, they soon declared their area in the Frontón jail a 'liberated zone'. No soldier or civilian, unless he was a member of the party, was allowed to enter their Blue Pavilion. Only bullets entered.

Father Lanssiers was the prison chaplain. His first task was to obtain mattresses for the prisoners who until then had slept on stone beds. He came up with the idea to telephone the recently elected president of Peru, Fernando Belaúnde. Lanssiers had no contacts and made no attempts to work through established channels. 'I didn't think much about my powers in those days.' He called the president's office directly and, incredibly, weeks later, he did reach the president. In a rage, Belaúnde ordered mattresses to be sent to Frontón because 'it's shameful that foreigners should be the ones who show concern for our own prisoners'.

But not all the authorities treated the chaplain so cordially. His incomprehensible concern for the terrorists and his constant warnings in newspaper articles about innocent people being jailed unjustly made people suspect he was a subversive. The navy obstructed him in every way it could, and the National Anti-Terrorism Department kept him under surveillance for years. If they still allowed him to visit jails, it was because he was the only one the *senderistas* would admit to their pavilions.

'So your relationship with the armed forces has always been tense?' I deliberately interrupted him.

'Anyone's relationship with armed people is usually tense. And in those days, the cops usually shot, almost as a hobby. They'd kill dogs, birds and sometimes people. One day they killed two prisoners. When the prosecutor and the judge went in to examine the bodies, they were held hostage. Then I was called in. I was worried because I'd left the car parked where it would be stolen, so I wanted to resolve the matter quickly. I said to the *senderistas*, "Just once, the prosecutor and the judge explain to the cops that people are not to be killed, and what do you do? You kidnap them. Are you crazy?"

'What they wanted was to perform their own rituals over the bodies, a liturgy much more complicated than the Catholic rite. "Comrade So-and-So, murdered by that dog Belaúnde, the Revolutionary Army will avenge you . . ." The comrades, wearing ski masks, would repeat each sentence nine times and give speeches against each of the functionaries. And if the functionaries tried to speak, they'd be silenced.

'I had to spend the whole night there to protect the officials. At about five in the morning, the *senderistas* began to debate whether they should return the bodies. Two more hours. Finally one came and said, "Comrade, we decided that we aren't going to return the bodies to the traitorous reactionaries . . . We're going to give them to you." All I could think was, "What luck that they're rather light." I carried them out and gave them back to the reactionaries. The car wasn't stolen but, of course, no one was punished for the murders.

'Another time, they took the entire administrative staff of the

National Penitentiary Institute prisoner. I'd get a call every night. That was in 1985. The next year, in July, the terrorists in the principal prisons all rioted at the same time. These were repressed using the quick method: in a single day, almost three hundred prisoners were murdered. The orders came directly from the government of Alan García.'

'Would you say then that President García was a murderer?'

'If I started condemning all the murderers I know, I'd have to find another line of work.'

That was strike two. I'd have to forget my headline and just try to listen.

'Father, have you ever felt fear?'

'Not really.'

'Why not?'

'I don't know. I think I lack imagination. In some situations I would have been smarter if I had been afraid.'

'What is the most lethal group you ever encountered?'

'The Khmer Rouge. They were irrational. The *senderistas* are irrational too, but they've changed. Now they have a sense of humour.'

'What if a group like the Khmer Rouge took power in Peru? Would you be afraid then?'

Lanssiers put out his last cigarette, which barely fitted into the ashtray. Everything seemed to suggest that he was finally going to express a feeling, perhaps even make a statement about values because, for the first time, he waited a few, almost imperceptible seconds, thinking over his answer.

'Yes, I'd be afraid. But I wouldn't leave. It's a matter of principle. In simple terms, you have to do something to keep people from one another. And often, all it takes is for enemies to get to know one another.'

After three hours of conversation, Lanssiers reached no conclusions, gave me no answers, resolved not one doubt. He eluded any question that implied an opinion and refused to say anything that wasn't a pure, direct narrative told with a total absence of emotion about the things he'd seen. I left his office with something too long to publish anywhere and with my head filled with things no one wanted to know.

I wrote the article but it was rejected even by the opposition newspapers and despite the information I managed to eke out of Lanssiers about the disappeared. The argument was that there was no 'hook' or angle to the story; it didn't fit in with the picture of Lanssiers. One of the editors suggested it would be better if I wrote about pretty girls on the beach. Something with nice photos.

Months later, on 11 October 2000, I left Peru.

I was living in Spain when I learned about Father Lanssiers' death. His two-pack-a-day cigarette habit wasn't the cause. He had died of a ruptured ulcer. At the request of the prisoners, the priest's coffin went to three jails, and in each it lay in state. Standing next to his coffin, terrorists, soldiers, rapists, ex-ministers, thieves and drug dealers all wept.

Many things have happened in Peru and the rest of the planet since then. Many terrorists have killed in the name of beautiful things like liberty or God. And many countries have invaded others in the name of democracy or freedom. Perhaps for that reason, I've come to share, more than ever, the sceptical neutrality of Father Hubert Lanssiers. When two groups willing to die for grand ideals face each other, the dead quickly bury the ideals. In one way or another, Deng's dogs are still hanging from the lamp posts of the world, and the only thing that changes is the colour of their cold fur. ∎

THE INFAMOUS BENGAL MING

Rajesh Parameswaran

The one clear thing I can say about Wednesday, the worst and most amazing day of my life, is this: it started out beautifully. I woke up with the summer dawn, when the sky goes indigo grey and the air's empty coolness begins to fill with a tacky, enveloping warmth. I could hear Saskia and Maharaj purring to each other at the far end of my compound. I'd had to listen to their cooing and screeching sex noises all night, but it didn't bother me. I didn't know why yet, but I realized: I was over it. Saskia could sleep with every tiger in the world but me, and I wouldn't mind.

I stretched and smacked my mouth and licked my lips, tasting the familiar odours of the day. Already, I somehow sensed that this morning would be different from all the other mornings of my life. On the far side of the wall hippos mucked and splashed, and off in the distance the monkeys and the birds who had been up since pre-dawn darkness started their morning chorus in earnest, their caws and kee-kees and caroo-caroo-caroos echoing out over the breadth of our little kingdom. These were the same sounds I heard morning after morning, but this morning it was all more beautiful than ever; yes, this morning was different. It took me a little while to puzzle out the reason, but once I did, it was unmistakable.

I was in love.

It wasn't with one of the tigers in my compound – no, I had exhausted the possibilities of our small society long ago and, other than Saskia, there hadn't been any new arrivals in years. In fact, the object of my love wasn't another tiger at all. I was in love with my keeper, Kitch.

I know it sounds strange. It kind of caught me by surprise, too, but there really wasn't any avoiding the conclusion.

And it was all the stranger because I had known Kitch for years. When I was a cub he had been something like an assistant to my first keepers. He wore wire-frame glasses then, and he was skinny and nervous. It was amusing to see him struggle to keep a clear path between himself and the compound door, in case he needed to make a quick escape! It's true what they say about us: we can smell fear, and that's why I noticed him. I was nervous around people then, too, and his manner piqued my particular interest.

Over the years, other keepers came and went, tigers disappeared and new ones arrived, but Kitch was always there. He grew a moustache. His cheeks got round and his belly filled out. His hair went thinner and thinner every time he took off his cap. He shaved his moustache. He lost the wariness that I had once found so intriguing.

His manner changed, his appearance changed, but he was always the same sweet Kitch. And that Wednesday I woke up and realized: Kitch. Kitch! I love Kitch. Realizing I loved Kitch was like realizing that a bone you have enjoyed chewing for months is actually the bone of your worst enemy. The bone hasn't changed, nor your enjoyment of it, but suddenly things are seen with a whole new perspective. Actually, that's a very negative example, but the point is this: I had just discovered a deep and endless love for the best friend I had ever had in my life.

I should probably clarify. This wasn't the sort of love like when you see a hot new cat and can't keep your claws off her. I didn't love Kitch like I had loved Saskia, not with the same, shall we say, roaring passion. This love wasn't as agitating.

This was a different love. Every morning, when the big metal doors opened in the fibreglass rock, and pound after pound of cow meat and fresh organs came slithering down the passageway, whose face was there in the dark distance, shovel in hand? Kitch's. When Maharaj growled and got restless and came looking for a fight, who was the first to hear his shrieky howls, to fire a water hose and scare him off me? Kitch. I was inexhaustibly interesting to him, and he was an inexhaustible curiosity and a comfort and joy to me.

I think I'd call that love.

And once I realized I loved Kitch, everything else in the world seemed to make so much perfect sense: Saskia rejecting me; the walls that contained me; lonely old ladies; little children eating caramel corns; cockatoos and monkeys; and everything under the sun, so weird and funny and strange. I had food and water and friends and Kitch. I really didn't need much more than this, did I?

It's a little embarrassing even to think back on how happy I felt. And it didn't take long for things to take a turn for the worse. The first sign was when I walked to the rock down which my food usually came slithering, leaving a trail of red, wet glisten. This morning I walked to the rock and looked up and waited. Nothing came. I sniffed and I waited. I closed my eyes and opened them.

No food. No Kitch.

I waited some more. And I waited and I waited. I started to play a game. I would shut my eyes for a few moments at a time, and while my eyes were closed I would convince myself that as soon as I opened them, the food would be there. I kept them closed for longer periods each time, but the food never arrived.

Now I was very hungry, and when I'm hungry my head hurts. In fact, it pounds. I shut my eyes firmly and tried to sleep it away, but the sun was quickly becoming unbearably hot and I didn't want to go in search of shade lest I miss the food when it finally came, and Maharaj, finished with his own meal but greedy still, would come and pilfer it.

So I lay down right there, under the sun, and tried to quiet the pounding in my head. By this time the people had started to arrive – not just a few early-morning walkers, but thick hordes of people, huge summer swarms, three or four deep, five or six herds of summer campers alone, plus tourists and regulars.

Normally, I don't mind the people who come to visit the zoo. They have their business, I have mine. They come, watch for a few minutes, point and stare, talk about me, eat their ice creams, whatever, I don't care. But today there were so many of them, and they were so loud, and I was so hungry and my head was pounding and I was just trying to relax, to stay calm and wait for my food, but they kept talking; and some little kid started to scream, 'Wake up! Wake up, tiger! Wake up!' And then a whole chorus of kids joined him. 'Wake up, tiger! Wake up!'

I might have been able eventually to block them out and fall asleep, but right then I smelled Saskia, and that smell made me perk up. She was walking directly towards me with that little sashay, that little walk of hers. I loved to contemplate the fluffy patch of white fur right beneath her tail, and the way her tail brushed over it lightly as she swayed from side to side to side. As I said, I was over her. I was totally fine with the idea of her together with Maharaj, fucking Maharaj. But that didn't mean I had to stop appreciating her walk, that didn't mean I was prohibited from inhaling a deep whiff of her gorgeous aroma as she walked towards me.

I purred to her, very casually. Just a 'Hello there, Saskia'. I waited for her to return the greeting but she didn't even look at me. She walked past me like I wasn't even there.

Now, this annoyed me. It's one thing for her to sleep with Maharaj. That's her business and her prerogative. But just to ignore me like that, as if we were no one to each other – that was too much. I felt a little stupid for having let myself get carried away with admiring her walk and everything, and just to show her that she had put me out of sorts, I snarled. It was a small snarl, accompanied by a little swat of my paw: a warning swat. There was no way I could have made contact. But when she saw me lift my paw, she jumped around and roared so loudly that I almost pissed right where I stood. All right, I actually did piss. Then she walked away as cool as could be.

I could hear the school kids laughing at me now, but I ignored them and curled around and lay down again. Then I heard a loud rustle in the bushes and I started to get nervous because it sounded like Maharaj. Maharaj is a healthy beast of a cat. He has almost three times my bulk, and he makes a lot of noise when he moves. He must have heard Saskia's growl and was coming to check out the situation.

Maharaj took his time, moving real slow, hefting his huge, heavy body through the brush, and I could smell him now – it was definitely

Maharaj, so the fear and the pressure were kind of building up inside me. I was debating: should I try to get away and risk attracting his attention; or should I sit still and stay as quiet as possible and hope he'd ignore me?

I decided to make a move for it, but this turned out to be the wrong decision. As soon as I got up and started to walk I heard Maharaj break into a run, and in three quick bounds – boom, boom, boom – his heavy body was on top of mine and his claws were in my back and his teeth were sunk deep into my ass.

I screamed and writhed, but he kept me pinned down for thirty seconds or a minute, during which time I heard him fart, casual, loud and stinky, as if to demonstrate how relaxed he was, how little effort it took him to keep me locked down and in pain. Finally, he released me, as calm as could be. He got up and started to walk away. (He didn't even look at me – just like Saskia.) He paused in front of the door in the rock where I usually got my food. Then he crouched down and sent out a fat stream of piss. The smell would stick to that rock for days, and he knew it.

At this point I was thinking: Kitch. I just want Kitch. I want him to show up and salvage this day and restore it to its original promise. I want Kitch to bring me my food and wash my rock. I want Kitch to hang around for a few minutes and keep Maharaj away from me. I want to hear Kitch's voice flattering me and telling me what a good and handsome cat I was and telling me what to do. Actually, it would have been fine if Kitch didn't do any of these things. He could have forgotten the food and said not a word to me, for all I cared. I just wanted him to be there.

I just wanted to see his face for a few seconds, just to look at him. In fact, just thinking about Kitch's pink face made me feel better, gave me a feeling of hope and calm, and made the throbbing in my ass and my head fade just a little. He would be here soon, I knew it.

I settled down again and closed my eyes. The noise of the crowd also settled, finally, into a distant hum and chatter like it usually did, like a sonic blanket over the world, and in a little while I managed to fall asleep.

When I woke up it was grey and cool, a bank of clouds having moved in over the sun. My headache was better, but now my whole torso ached from hunger. I sniffed around the metal door, but there was still nothing there but the odour of Maharaj's cat piss.

Kitch still hadn't arrived. I couldn't believe it.

At that moment, I heard a familiar noise wafting over the moat that separated me from the visitors.

The river is chilly and the river is cold, Hallelujah
Michael, row the boat ashore, Hallelujah.

Oh God, I thought. Not the 'row-your-boat' lady, not today of all days. She sat down on the bench, sweatered and stinking, hair astray, grinning with her broken teeth. I could smell her from where I sat!

I roared at her instinctively, but she didn't shut up. In fact, she let out a whoop and a holler and sang all the louder.

The river is deep and the river is wide, Hallelujah
Milk and honey on the other side, Hallelujah.

I got up and paced back and forth, pausing every now and again to glare, but she wasn't intimidated in the least. She sang and she sang and she sang. After maybe half an hour, the singing faded into soft, incoherent chatter, until finally she slumped low on the bench and started to snore.

Still the day dragged on, and the sun had barely even crested in the sky. I felt a painful knock! knock! knock! in my head, and looked up and saw the teenaged zoo attendant banging his litter stick against the bench, trying to rouse the row-your-boat lady. Finally, she woke up and walked quietly away.

Kitch, I kept thinking. Kitch Kitch Kitch Kitch Kitch.

And just then, I saw Maharaj rising over the hill again, moving steady and fast, fairly bristling for another confrontation. What had I done this time? I kept repeating Kitch's name like a mantra. My head was about to explode into a million little pieces. It hurt so bad I could barely move it from one side to the other, and Maharaj was moving in for the kill, ready to carve up my rump and shit on my lair for good measure. And just at that moment, just as the pressure in my head was reaching the point where my brains felt like they would liquefy and boil and shoot from my ears in jets of steam, just as Maharaj crouched down for the pounce, just as all these things were about to happen, the people door creaked open and who was there but Kitch!

It was really him, his face aglow in the sunlight, and I almost jumped into the air with delight. Maharaj turned and galloped away to hide. The pain in my head melted into some pink, loving bliss. Where was my hunger? Where was all the gloom and trouble of the day? It was all gone. Kitch was here!

I paced back and forth and miaowed. I ran around in a circle and bit my tail. I peed in a long hot stream with a big grin on my face. I paced up and down and up and down again, and then I rolled on my back and let my tongue loll out. Then I popped upright and roared. It was Kitch! Yes, Kitch was here! And I loved him! And he was here!

Little did I know the most horrible thing was yet to happen.

Kitch was still standing near the door. In fact, he seemed, for some reason, unnaturally cautious. He hadn't advanced towards me at all, nor had he called out to return my greetings, and that's when I realized there was someone with him – an older man with thick glasses, wearing white rubber gloves on his hands. Kitch began, finally, to walk to one side of me, slowly, while trying to shield this other, nervous, man from my view.

Well, I had no time for this nonsense. Kitch was here, and I was hungry, and I had something to tell him. I loved him, and my love couldn't contain itself, and I wanted to make Kitch feel it, too. I pranced right up to Kitch, to just about three feet away from him, as close as I had ever been.

I'm here, Kitch, I meant to say; and I love you.

When I jumped forward like this, the man with glasses behind Kitch gripped Kitch's shoulder hard and said something I couldn't quite hear, and Kitch yelled at me sharply. And then Kitch did something I couldn't believe. He had a long stick in his hand – he always carried it, but I'd never seen him use it before. Now he raised this long stick high above his head and brought it down hard on my nose.

I yowled and backed away, stunned. At first, I couldn't understand what had happened. There was a sharp, reverberating pain between my eyes; the world before me seemed to split into two or three identical sharp-edged versions of itself, and then everything became clouded in hazy splotches of red.

Slowly, my senses returned to me. I began to realize what had happened, that Kitch had actually hit me, that he had hit me hard in front of this new person. But why? What had I done? I had only been trying to show how much I loved him.

Now, I began to feel very bad – not just the pain in my nose, but a different, difficult kind of anguish. Why would Kitch do a thing like that? Didn't he appreciate me? After I had wanted nothing more all day than to see that beautiful fat face and to love him, even though he had ignored me since yesterday, even though he had left me all alone and hadn't bothered even to feed me? All that love he could have had for the taking, but instead he'd gone and done a thing like this: he'd hit me! I was embarrassed and ashamed, and my ears began to run hot with blood. And then I began to feel angry.

And all at once the anger welled up inside me, filling me like a hot liquid, and before I knew what was happening, I took a huge leap and tackled Kitch. We fell down with a hard bang to the ground, and my claws held him fast – and in a way, it felt good to hold him like that, a powerful kind of feeling. And then I bit him, just once, hard and quick.

It happened so fast, and it wasn't at all intentional. At least I don't think it was intentional. It didn't feel intentional, but to be honest, it didn't quite feel accidental either. It was somewhere in between. I was on him and I bit him – just once – and then I stepped away, all in the blink of an eye.

The old man behind him screamed and retreated behind the people door and then I blinked and looked down at where Kitch was lying.

I had bitten him on the neck, and I saw there were two round, black holes where my teeth had entered him. And now two thick streams of blood began to spout out of those holes. Kitch was staring at me with a concerned look, and his mouth was moving up and down, and now blood was coming out of his mouth as well.

I couldn't quite believe what I was seeing. Just a few seconds ago Kitch had been standing up and healthy and I had been so happy to see him, and now he was lying on the ground and blood was spilling out of his mouth because of something I had done. This hadn't happened. This couldn't be happening. I had never hurt anyone in all my life. I didn't even know I had the power to take a man down so deftly. The blood was spreading black and wet around him.

Now, I knew I had to put a stop to this. I had to reverse whatever this was that had happened. I ran up to Kitch, and I saw that he was scared of me now. I licked his neck from where the blood was coming and tried to make the blood stop. Kitch feebly pushed and tried to kick at me, but I ignored him and kept licking. I licked and I licked, but the blood kept pouring out, and so I licked faster.

And as I licked for what seemed like minutes, I slowly became conscious of the fact that there was no way my licking was going to stop this blood from pouring out. And yet I couldn't stop licking. I didn't want to stop licking, because another surprising realization was forming in the back of my mind, something that had never even remotely occurred to me before, a realization that made me want to lick and lick faster, and keep licking forever. The realization was:

Kitch's blood was delicious.

As soon as this thought formed itself in my mind, I jumped back in horror. This was Kitch's blood I was drinking. Kitch, whom I loved! What was I doing?

I turned around to look for help. Saskia and Maharaj were standing at a distance, staring with eager curiosity, but neither of them made the slightest move to help me. I knew they were too cautious to get involved, and I couldn't be bothered to convince them.

I looked then to the other side of the moat, where dozens and dozens of people were staring at us and talking and pointing in alarm. One of these people could surely help Kitch, I thought. I ran up and down and roared, and tried to get their attention, but none of them made the first effort to cross the moat and help us. In fact, some of them started to throw things at me – paper cups full of soda, little rocks – and some of them started to yell. To hell with them, I thought. When I turned back around to check on Kitch, I saw that the old man with glasses was crouched down and trying to do something to my friend. Was the old man helping? Was someone helping at last? I ran back to check, but as soon as I did, the old man fell backwards and stumbled hurriedly out of the people door, leaving it swinging wildly behind him.

Poor Kitch! Nobody would help him. His eyes were open and he was pale. The blood from his neck had slowed to a trickle and the ground around him was soggy like after a three-day rain. His lips were moving so slightly, and then they stopped moving, and his eyes just stared up. I licked his sweet face, but he didn't respond. Oh Kitch! What had I done? I had to find help for him if it was the last thing I did. I turned and ran out of the people door. I had never been past this door before, but I didn't think twice about it. I went through the door, down a narrow passage, and was outside.

There were hundreds of people all around – literally hundreds – but why wouldn't any of them stop to help me? They all ran away, as if terribly frightened of something, everywhere I looked. What mysterious terror could have overtaken the zoo's entire human population, on this day of all days? What could be so terrible that it would keep them from helping Kitch? Had an elephant escaped?

The situation finally became clear to me: I was Kitch's only hope. I ran back to the door of my compound but as soon as I got there I saw a bright flash and heard a blast. When the smoke cleared and my ears stopped ringing, I saw that a tall, thin man had kneeled down very quietly behind the popcorn stand across from my compound. He held a long gun in his hands. He had been waiting for me, apparently, and now he fired again.

I crouched down and stayed very still. He fired a third time, and I heard a loud crash behind me. I tried to lunge towards him but then he fired once more, and the blast was so close that my face burned with its heat, and I had no choice but to turn around and run.

I ran and I ran, and the people around me screamed and ran too, and I ran behind these people, and I ran alongside them, having nowhere else to go; and finally I ran away from them. I kept running until I had no idea where I was any more. There were no animals and no people: just a long ribbon of black, with objects rushing by, things on wheels that groaned and squawked and growled. Every few minutes I heard – or thought I heard – the crash and fire of the tall man's rifle that had almost burned me moments earlier, and then I ran even harder. I ran alongside those fast-rolling things, and they swerved and smashed and croaked and honked. I kept running and running, not sure where I was headed, just desperate to get away from the madness that had become my life, and hoping still to find some help, somehow, for Kitch.

I ran until I could barely pick up my legs any longer, and each breath raked my lungs with sharpened claws. I slowed down and looked around and saw that the rolling objects had grown, finally, sparse and distant. I saw wide grassy expanses, and small houses set back nicely on the neat grass. Everywhere I looked: houses and grass, nicely spaced, as far as the eye could see. And this vista, the longest vista I could remember ever having seen, stirred me with a strange exhilaration. I could run as long and as far as I wanted here, with no wall to stop me! And I did run. As tired as I was, something in my heart stirred me to run again, in great leaping strides. It was a strange feeling – to be on the run; to be worried about Kitch, whom I had hurt; to be away from the only home I had known, and yet to feel this strange and almost terrifying euphoria. On one of these great lawns, behind a small house, I was gratified to see a huge ice-blue pool of water. I stopped here and drank as much water as I could hold. Then I put my very head into the pool and lifted it out, sopping and cold. And now the pull of sleep was overwhelming, so I sank down where I was and closed my eyes.

But the sleep was brief and fitful. On the backs of my eyelids, I saw again the image of Kitch bleeding and gasping on the ground; I saw the man with thick glasses and rubber gloves, reaching those gloved hands towards me. I saw Maharaj and Saskia, staring at all this with strange glee on their faces. Finally, I heard the soft steps of the man with the rifle, and heard the sharp lightning of his gun and I woke up with a start.

Was he really nearby, or had that been part of the dream? The wide-open vista, which a few moments before had brought me a feeling of elation, now seemed fraught with danger. I was too exposed here. That quiet man with his long gun was probably this moment lining me up in his sights.

The pool where I had drunk sat right behind a small house or building, and I crept up to it and sniffed for any danger. It was hard to smell anything in this place, but an odour of humans seemed to linger in the air, like it did at the zoo, wafting from a distance; and this smell reminded me of the comfort of my home. I pushed and shoved at the glassy doors of the building until I found an access that gave at my pressure and, quietly, I stepped inside.

The house was shadowy and silent, and walking on the soft, furry floors, I came to a cave-like room, dark and quiet and cool, and here, for the first time, I fell asleep and slept so that I forgot myself, for a short time at least.

I woke up well rested, and eager to resume searching out some help for Kitch. But when I opened my eyes I saw that the room was brightly lit, not dark as it had been earlier. There were coloured pictures on the wall: red-nosed clowns carrying motley balloons, just like I had seen some days in the zoo. On one side of the room was an open-topped cage raised on small stilts, and from inside the cage came the strangely calming sounds of a murmuring human cub – again, another sound I was well used to hearing in my home.

But before I noticed any of these things, of course, I noticed the woman standing across the room from me. She was a full-grown human, with brown curly hair and pink skin, like Kitch's skin. Her back was against the wall and she was inching towards the cub's cage with small sideways steps.

I lifted my head from my paws, my nose quivering with excitement, my ears and the hair on my back rigid with attention. When she saw me perk up, the woman paused where she was standing and took a sharp breath inward. Her arms were spread behind her, and her fingers were splayed backwards with their tips resting against the wall. She seemed to force herself to breathe again with great, trembling deliberation. Finally, she released the wall and began to walk once more, slowly, towards the cage.

A cat has an instinct for such situations, and my instinct quickly told me: this woman was mother to the crying cub. Normally, I would have thought that she'd be a threat to me only insofar as she would try to protect her offspring, but my recent experiences had warned me that humans were dangerously unpredictable, and I had better be careful of her regardless.

I rose and stepped, very slowly, in a direction opposite to the direction that the woman was walking – that is, I walked away from the cub's cage – and the woman stalked carefully towards her cub, and like that we circled the room warily.

The baby human was murmuring in the softest, most innocent way, and in fact I wanted this mother to take it and care for it. Like most cats in the zoo, I considered myself an orphan: where I came from, who my mother was, I have no recollection. But as I walked that strange duet with this cautious human mother, I had a brief and visceral flash of an older female tiger, a warm and orange-coloured softness, a light and muscular embrace. I felt my legs quiver beneath me, and then I had another brief flash of memory: a strong blow to the face, like the blow that Kitch had given me; a fast run through the brush, a panic of voices.

Now I felt dizzy with strange emotion. And that human woman must have sensed my unsteadiness. She took the opportunity to move quickly towards her own cub, and with arms shaking terribly, she reached inside and pulled out the gurgling thing.

Her sudden movement brought me back to my senses. I turned swiftly, to keep track of her actions, and when she saw me move like that, the woman let out a terrifying shriek; and in her panic she allowed her little one to slip right from out of her hands.

What happened next happened so quickly I can barely describe it. I saw the fleshy child tumble towards the ground, and in one instinctive surge I lunged towards it.

The next thing I knew, the tiny human dangled, upside down and crying, from my mouth; I held it only by the crinkled piece of cloth it wore around its bottom.

The mother stood a few feet away from me, and she cried out now even more uncontrollably than her cub did, and her cheeks were flushed bright orange. I had never seen a human so upset before, and I had no idea how she would behave now.

I started to move forward, thinking I would return her offspring to her, but as soon as I lifted my paw to move, she yelled and quivered more alarmingly than before, so I stepped back again.

Now I really had no idea what to do. I couldn't move in any direction without sending the woman into further hysterics. I just stood there blankly.

When it began to seem that our terrible, nervous stalemate might last forever, this woman ended it in a totally surprising way. She bent down to her knees and picked up a couple of coloured wooden blocks. She got up and flung them at me hard.

The blocks hit me sharply on the flank, and I backed off into a crouch. The woman seemed to get her courage back when she saw me cower. She started to pick up anything she could get her hands on – plastic things on wheels, blocks of many colours, soft and furry shapes resembling bears and lions and people – and she rained these objects on me in a continuous, angry hail.

As soon as I got over my surprise I began to realize that as hard as she threw these objects, they didn't really hurt me. And more often than not, they hit wide of their mark. Frankly, I was more concerned that, with her wild arm, she would hit her own cub – and in fact this happened: even as I tried to curl around and protect it, a high-flying train flew over my head and bounced off the piss-wet leg of the little one.

Now I was thoroughly annoyed. I let the cub drop softly to the pillowy floor and turned around and roared at the mother with all the might of my hot and humid lungs. Then I stepped towards her and roared again as loud as I was able to.

As I said, humans are so unpredictable. As soon as I roared like this, the curly-haired lady collapsed as instantly and softly as a pile of feathers from a startled bird. She fell to the ground in a dead faint.

After a few seconds, I gathered the courage to approach her inert body. I bent down, sniffed her, licked her face, but she didn't wake up.

Now what was I to do? The cub had begun roaring, wailing and crying, rolling this way and that on the floor. It didn't seem right to leave it there so helpless, with its mother lying unconscious. I went back to the little one and sniffed it. I had thought that Maharaj was an ugly-smelling beast, but this human cub smelled terrible. I licked its pudgy, salty face, but this had no comforting effect. Finally, I picked it up again by its soiled cloth.

I pushed my way back out the door through which I had entered the house earlier. I went to the ice-blue pool where I had enjoyed such a refreshing drink a few hours previously, and I held the baby human's face to the cool water, thinking perhaps it was thirsty.

But it didn't reach for the water – in fact, it seemed a little frightened of it. So I took the liberty of dipping its face into the liquid, ever so gently. But now the little thing coughed and spat, and began crying all the louder.

With this loud crying, my pounding headache from earlier that morning began to creep back. I also worried that these loud noises would draw the attention of the neighbouring people, or of the man with the rifle, who I was sure, even then, was stalking me. I thought to leave the little one there and run away, but I couldn't bear the thought of this helpless, undefended, motherless cub in the open. Really, something had to be done, and quickly, to quiet this confounding little human. I admit I don't have the instincts of a mother, and for a long time I had no idea what to do.

Then I had a stroke of inspiration. I lay the cub down softly on the grassy lawn. I opened my mouth wide and took its whole head, gently, inside my own mouth, and in this way I picked it up again.

There! The sound of the cub's crying was considerably muffled. My mouth also provided a kind of warm and comforting womb for it. And soon, in fact, the flailing arms and legs of the little one stopped moving, the cries in my mouth softened into comforted whimpers, and finally into silence as it drifted to sleep.

Only when I released the cub's head and laid him gently out on the grass again did I realize what I had done. Yes, the baby human had stopped crying, but it had stopped breathing, too! I had stupidly, inadvertently, recklessly suffocated it. Oh God. I picked it up and shook it left and right. I dropped it down and roared at it and then picked it up and swung it about some more, hoping somehow to wake it.

By the time I had finished, the cub was no more alive than it had been when I started, but its body was considerably worse for wear, with little rips here and there, dislocated joints, bruises spreading like swollen lakes, and puncture marks everywhere, most upsettingly (for me) in its right eye, which dribbled a colourful syrup.

I felt sick to my stomach. How did I keep doing this – time after time – killing people unintentionally? What was wrong with me? Was I evil?

I picked the human up again by its filthy cloth, this limp little human whose head I had crushed, and carried it away with me, dangling from my teeth. Now I had two people to fix, and I was comforted by this notion at least: If I could find someone to help me fix this cub (who was light and easy to carry), then I would know there was hope for Kitch. (And, yes, I couldn't help but taste the blood of this human; it tasted even sweeter than Kitch's blood. But even though I had eaten nothing for a full day, the thought never crossed my mind to eat this child. To be precise, it crossed my mind only once, but I quickly put the sick notion out of my head.)

I walked through the streets of that place, dangling that dead, dripping human baby before me like the nightwatchman in the zoo carried a lamp in the dark, and I saw no other creature. There was no one who could help.

I must have walked another quarter day until I reached a vast sea of resting vehicles, and a large building that was thronged with people. I walked towards this throng – and again, people screamed and ran away from me – but by now I was so inured to this reaction that I simply ignored it. I was looking for that one person who would see me and stop and know what to do – that person who would know how to help this cub and to help me and to help my friend – my love – Kitch.

I pushed my way into the building and people yelled and ran away from me in every direction, but I calmly walked forward. People carried bags of clothes, of toys, of devices and things, and they dropped and flung these bags in every direction as they saw me, but I simply and calmly walked.

When I reached the other end of the building, I stepped outside again into the sunlight. No one had helped me and I wondered, really, did nobody care for a dead baby? Was there nobody in this world who cared?

By this point, the sun was sinking low in the sky and I was depressed. I just wanted to lie down and forget everything, I wanted to unwind this day and let it disappear into nothing.

I found my way across another avenue – the vehicles screeched and crashed and almost hit me, but I didn't care – and I found a quiet corner beneath a large bridge. Above me I could hear those fast-rolling vehicles, but down here it was dark and cool and quiet. I set the human cub carefully down and I lay beside it. Far in the distance, I heard those wild howling sirens. The objects whooshed and whooshed overhead, and the bridge shivered and clanked with their weight. From somewhere in the sky came the cluttered drone of objects flying and every sound in this world seemed ugly and new. In the distance, I thought I heard the loud report of a rifle, and I knew that the orange fire of that gun was near in my future. I wanted nothing else but to be back in my enclosure, and for the baby to be alive, and for Kitch to be OK again. But I knew it would never happen. I had been kidding myself – nothing in the world could bring Kitch back to life. Certain things can never be reversed.

I thought of Kitch's pudgy face as it had been a few days ago: bright and pink beneath his khaki cap, and a smile settled on my face. I remembered the cooing noises of the row-your-boat lady singing her sad song. It had annoyed me so, but now that noise seemed so lovely.

My brothers and sisters are all aboard, Hallelujah
Michael, row the boat ashore, Hallelujah.

And the noise was so close and so real that I thought she could have been there right beside me, singing, and when I looked up, she was. It would have surprised me to see her there on any other day, but this day nothing surprised me any more. She was sitting beneath the same bridge as I was, amid a nest of bags and garbage. She looked at me and sang and smiled through her broken teeth.

Then she got up and walked right up to me. 'You came all the way here to see me, tiger?' she asked me.

I was too tired to get up but I raised my head slightly. I was so happy to see her that tears were streaming from my eyes.

She saw the human baby lying next to me, and she shook her head. 'Oh, tiger,' she said. 'Oh, that's a shame.' She bent down and stroked the top of the cub's head. 'Ming the merciless!' she whooped, and then she started to chuckle to herself, and that laugh was the strangest, sweetest sound I had ever heard.

I closed my eyes. And saw the zoo and its miniature red-green forest, and it was full of tigers, just like me. And Saskia and Maharaj were there, and I had forgiven them and I ran and I played with them. And the baby's curly-haired mother stood nearby, but she was my mother, too – she had been my mother all along. And in my dream, I had my own kids, baby tigers, playful little cubs, as small as I had been once, just as small as the human baby I had killed. The tiger babies tumbled over each other clumsily, so cute. I tried to lick them and play with them, but I saw that my tongue and my paws were rough and too powerful, and the slightest touch would have damaged those babies, so I stopped playing, and instead I stood guard and watched over them.

On the other side of the moat, Kitch and great hordes of humans watched and admired; and then, one by one they started to climb over the wall, and wade through the moat – so eager were they to reach us. Soon, great armies of people were crossing over into the tiger compound, and they came running up my hill. There were so many of them that I couldn't protect my delicate babies from their heavy feet. They trampled right over my cubs, mashing them down in their oblivious rush, and the strange old man with thick glasses and rubber gloves came around and picked up my dead babies and dropped them into a plastic bag and I was distraught. But then Kitch came to me. He stopped and patted me on the head, and scratched me behind the ear. He told me it was OK. He said the tiger babies were gone and it was OK, and he was gone, and that was OK, too. And I realized that as he petted me he was beginning to crush my head, like wet sludge in his hand. His fingers were deep in my brain, and he was massaging it into a pulp and it felt good, in a way, but it terrified me also, because I knew I would soon be lost in oblivion.

When I woke up, it was dark. I had the aching hunger that stretched my ribs. The droning noise from the sky was harder and closer, and I knew soon I would have to get up and keep moving to stay out of reach of the rifles. But at that second, the thought didn't bother me. I had that morning feeling again, that feeling I had when I first realized that I loved Kitch, and the world had made a brief and wonderful kind of sense.

Everything seemed so clear again, everything that was horrible was sensible, and everything was good, and I understood it all. I looked down and saw that the row-your-boat lady had fallen asleep with her head resting on top of me. She was curled into a ball, with her head nestled right up against my haunches, as peaceful as could be, and I thought, she is a wonderful person. I love you, row-your-boat lady, I said to myself, as I opened my mouth wide and worked my teeth into her soft stomach and pulled up her viscera.

She gasped just once, without even opening her eyes – sharp and sudden as if she had just had a wonderful surprise. And then she stopped, never exhaling.

It felt so right, killing her like that. It moved me. I didn't do it from anger or from hunger; nor was it an act of recklessness, like with that poor little human baby. A word that comes to mind is *instinct*; and yet I know I chose to kill her. I chose to kill her, and it felt inevitable, and it made me sad and happy all at once. I set myself to my work, and when I had ripped out and eaten every organ and every sweet strip of flesh that I could peel from the row-your-boat lady, when I had sucked down even the soft rounds of meat in the cheeks of her face, when she was just a shiny hub of bone and muscle, I turned around and picked up the human cub. It took me just two bites to crunch and pop and slurp and swallow the whole thing, and I was crying as I did so. I had never felt so much love in all my life. ■

THE GROUND FLOOR

Daniel Alarcón

I met Darin Rossi standing in a thick, gooey pool of fake blood, on an early-December night in Los Angeles. He wore a striped umpire's uniform and had the beefy look of a lapsed athlete entering middle age: thick chest and neck, black hair gelled with heavy brilliantine and combed straight back. We were both waiting in a slow-moving line for the bathroom, between fights at the inaugural event of a crypto-gothic fight club called the Foam Weapon League (FWL). We made small talk, discussed other fight clubs we'd seen. I squished my sneakers against the floor and felt them stick. He did the same, and we laughed. Even the organizers had been unprepared for this detail – there was so much fake blood! After each fight – or were they battles? – the assistants got down on hands and knees to wipe the floor as clean as they could with gobs of thin paper towels. Everything was improvised. How hard would it have been to buy a mop?

Rossi didn't mind. He'd once been a Major League Baseball umpire, but since the early 2000s had transitioned into a career in film, television and commercials, playing an umpire. He blew his whistle with the confidence of a professional. Did he miss it – the real thing?

Rossi shook his head. 'Everyone hates the ump.'

Of course – any sports fan knows it.

He went on: 'Too much travel. Acting is way better.' He rattled off the names of a dozen productions he'd been a part of – *Bad News Bears*, *Coach Carter*, *The Longest Yard*, *Superman Returns*. In each case, he'd played a referee. Apparently he wasn't concerned with being typecast. For this gig with the FWL, his character was named Rossi the Regulator, and he even wore his old Major League pads under his black-and-white shirt, for extra bulk. He was hoping, he said, 'to get in on the ground floor'.

It's one of those uniquely American phrases that connotes a certain desperation, at least in my mind; a phrase that one imagines flying from the lips of a salesman looking feverishly for investors. A huckster might say it, or a swindler, but the romance of it is self-evident: the ground floor is where the real money is made. Buying in early, before the rest of the world has realized that what is being pawned is pure gold – that's what daring, hungry Americans do. The sad reality is that more often than not the ground floor is the only floor and my sense, after watching a hapless hour and a half of the FWL, was that this was the case now. Unexploded blood packs kept falling off contestants' vests; the fights were short, fitful and not particularly exciting. Two oddly dressed warriors with plastic swords flailing wildly at one another – it was brutish, simple and disappointing. All atmospherics, but no content. *This* was the ground floor?

L os Angeles – not the real city, but the version of that city that exists in the popular imagination – is a glamorous, glittering place of palm trees and movie stars. The actual city, which I've come to know just a bit over the course of many visits, is at once more interesting and superficially much less attractive. I'd go so far as to say there is no glamour at all remaining in the city itself, but only in its reflected image. It is a quality that tourists themselves import, something created spontaneously when out-of-towners photograph the names engraved on the sidewalks of Hollywood Boulevard, or crowd the windows of a boutique on Rodeo Drive, straining to see some second-rate starlet try on a pair of overpriced shoes. These attractions – if they could be called that – are collectively created works of fantasy; delusions beautiful in the way that all brands of faith are, made perhaps more poignant because, in the entire history of film, praying to a movie star has not yet produced a single documented miracle.

The rest of the city – its millions of residents, in thousands of mostly glum residential neighbourhoods – is essentially unknowable. Like many cities, Los Angeles has reached a size beyond which there can be any explaining. It is impossibly large, perfectly confounding, and absolutely surreal. No statement about the city can be made whose opposite would not also be true. The beach you see on television is, for most city-dwellers, a rumour. The mountains and canyons, too. Long, straight, featureless avenues like the one where the FWL held its inaugural event – these are legion. They stretch hundreds of blocks long, east to west, crossing elevations, climactic regions, time zones. Downtown looms. You arrive, only to find it empty. At noon, the smog hangs low and fetid, but if you look straight up the sky is still blue: a good, old-fashioned mirage. Quite unexpectedly, you smell the ocean, but it's still miles away.

It goes without saying that most of the contestants were actors. Or models. Or somehow connected to the behemoth industry that defines Los Angeles to the world and to itself. I knew this without needing to be told: it was apparent in the way these costumed men and women preened for the many cameras, apparent in the overheard chatter, anxious talk of agents and auditions and workshops. On the surface, the evening could have taken place in any American city – a curious group of eccentrics getting together to role-play on a weekend – what could be more wholesome? But in Los Angeles, it was that and something more: a way to build one's résumé, an experience that, with a little luck, would turn into a job.

That night at least, the possibilities felt real. The room was pregnant with dreams of stardom. There were signs along the walls, at the doors, that said FILMING IN PROGRESS. Rossi told me a few cable channels had shown interest, and talks about a pilot were in the works. The prospect was exciting, of course: his friend and fellow FWL referee had once been a regular on the show *Gladiators*, and it had paid well enough. I nodded. I liked Darin Rossi very much; there was an earnestness to him I found charming, all the more because it seemed so at odds with his career choice. He'd rather pretend to be something than actually be it. It was less risky, less arduous and probably paid better: *I'm not an umpire, but I play one on TV.*

Possibly less honest was Rossi's statement about his next project, which was, according to him, 'a film with Reese Witherspoon'.

About the FWL: how to describe the sensation of standing in the smallish front room of what was, by all appearances, an abandoned warehouse, drinking beer from a can and surrounded by men and women of all races, sizes, shapes and ages who'd come out this Saturday evening dressed as demons and cavemen, ninjas and wizards, escaped inmates, cartoon characters and the like? How to describe the disconcerting pleasure of it, the discovery, the sound of blood packs bursting, spilling their contents, the sight of the sticky red liquid spreading across the rutted cement and pooling in the fine cracks? How to describe the silliness of it? The farce? The man whose entire face and shaved dome were tattooed solid black, as if it were the helmet of a Roman soldier, and him screaming into a camera, the veins in his neck stretched taut and popping like tensely coiled rope?

I stood surrounded by monsters – whether their intention was to frighten or amuse wasn't clear.

The fights Rossi and his partner officiated were stylized battles between real-life avatars, characters created especially for the occasion. Their names were evocative, as were the costumes: Hardcore (tight black shorts, bare chest, the aforementioned tattooed face); Cavewoman (just like she sounds, adorned with a missing front tooth, for authenticity's sake); Arkon (think dark wizard). And there were others: The Squid; The Butch-Dyke; The Hammer; Big Bertha; and Three-Pac, who looked not like the rapper his name referenced, but like a deranged version of Bamm Bamm from *The Flintstones*. These were men who'd read comic books, perhaps studied them; women who'd spent hours staring at computers back when the one-colour screens showed only text and featured a cursor flashing like a hospital monitor showing a beating heart. It was all very playful, but also deadly serious and, except for a young Asian-American man decked out in all white playing a character he called 'Arctic' (whom the crowd adopted and re-baptized 'Kung-fu Panda'), there was no irony. Two of his drunker fans snuggled up to him and pronounced themselves proud members of 'Team Asia'. They posed with him, flashing peace signs; Arctic winced, but let himself be photographed anyway. Then he went out and slashed up Cavewoman. He was merciless. She never stood a chance.

I spent a few minutes talking with a narrow-faced man who introduced himself as Phil and asked for help pinning back the sleeves of his oversized black robe. He had a shaggy look to him, with stringy, light brown hair and a goatee that had not quite filled out. He had an advantage over the other competitors, he said: he was a martial arts instructor and worked with weapons all day. He spoke these last words boldly, stretching out the phrase 'all day' for emphasis. When I asked him about his character, Phil said, 'I'm the Angry Monk.'

He didn't seem particularly angry, I thought, but before I could point this out, Phil corrected himself. It was sudden, as if he'd just recalled the story he'd invented for the evening: 'Angry Ex-Monk, I should say, since I murdered my whole family.'

He didn't smile, so I didn't either, but instead tried to imagine what this timid, thoughtful man's family might have looked like, and how exactly he might have killed them. He probably hadn't made up that part of the story yet.

'How about that?' I said.

Across the room, Hardcore shouted into a digital video camera, fierce, violent, terrifying, his mouth open wide like the jaws of a raging beast. It was a guttural, nonsensical roar, one I imagine he'd practised in front of a mirror.

Even Angry Ex-Monk seemed shaken by the sight. He became Phil again, and nodded at the spectacle across the room. 'That'd be really scary if he wasn't acting.'

Or was it more scary because he was? ■

The Instructions *Adam Levin*

Gurion Maccabee, age ten: scholar, fighter and spectacular talker. Expelled from three schools for acts of violence and messianic tendencies, Gurion is in the Cage, a special lockdown programme. But in just four days, from meeting the beautiful Eliza June Watermark to the terrifying Events of November 17, Gurion's search for righteousness sparks a violent, unstoppable rebellion. *The Instructions* is hilarious, troubling, empathetic, monumental, breakneck, romantic and unforgettable.
Canongate £20 | HB

The Brain is Wider Than the Sky: Why Simple Solutions Don't Work in a Complex World *Bryan Appleyard*

Bryan Appleyard argues that it is time to resist handing over our lives to databases, iPads and smartphones, that we are more than 'simply' the product of our genetic make-up, and through art and literature we can reclaim the full depth of human experience. Complexity is our best defence. Exclusive cover by David Hockney.
Weidenfeld & Nicolson £20 | HB

Unpacking My Library – Writers and Their Books Edited by *Leah Price*

As words and stories are increasingly disseminated through digital means, the significance of the book as object – whether pristine collectible or battered relic – is growing too. *Unpacking My Library* spotlights the libraries of thirteen novelists. More than 200 colour photographs provide views of the libraries and close-ups of individual volumes.
Yale University Press £16 | HB

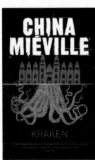

Kraken *China Miéville*

Deep in the research wing of the Natural History Museum, a perfect giant squid specimen mysteriously disappears. For curator Billy Harrow, it's the start of a headlong pitch into a London he's woefully unprepared for. Three-time winner of the Arthur C. Clarke Award, China Miéville creates a dark alternative vision of our world.
Pan Macmillan | PB

INSATIABLE

Mark Doty

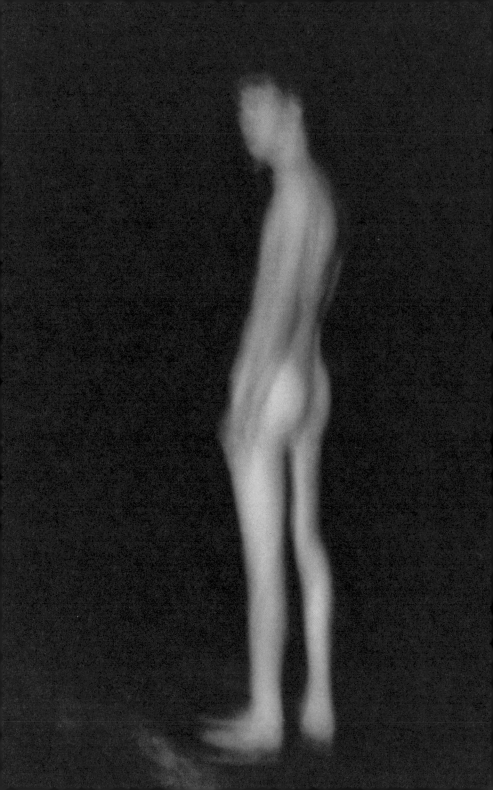

I only hope we may sometime meet and I shall be able perhaps to say what I cannot write.
  – Bram Stoker to Walt Whitman, February 1876

You did well to write to me so unconventionally, so fresh, so manly, & so affectionately.
  –Walt Whitman to Bram Stoker, March 1876

O nly a sentence, casually placed as a footnote in the back of Justin Kaplan's thick 2003 biography of Walt Whitman, but it goes off like a little explosion: 'Bram Stoker based the character of Dracula on Walt Whitman.'

Come again? The quintessential poet of affirmation, singer of himself, celebrant of human vitality – what has he to do with the parasitical phantom, the children of the night? The poet of 'Song of Myself' proclaims his solar confidence; he out gallops stallions, is 'plumb in the uprights' and 'braced in the beams' and even the smell of his own sweat famously delights him with 'an aroma finer than prayer'.

He seems himself a kind of sun, radiant, generous, aglow with an inner heat that seems composed of equal parts lust, good health and fellow feeling.

How could the embodiment of lunar pallor emerge from him?

W hat thrilled Whitman was vitality, and Bram Stoker – who'd been championing the older man's poems since his days at Trinity College, where he read them 'with my door locked late at night' – must have sensed this. He first found the expurgated edition that William Michael Rossetti had published in England, then ordered an American edition of *Leaves of Grass*, and proceeded to write Whitman a fan letter – really more of an outcry – about finding in the poems a kindred soul. 'I thank you for all the love and sympathy you have given me, in common with my kind,' Stoker wrote, and one can't help but read 'my kind' in a number of ways, which surely must have been what Stoker intended. The letter – a longish late-adolescent gush, which seems practically to fall over itself with hesitation, throat-clearing and a tumult of feeling – was charged enough for its author that he didn't manage to get it into the post for four years, which must place it right up there in the history of delayed correspondence. Whitman wrote an immediate reply; he was charmed by the letter and the note Stoker sent with it. Who wouldn't be, by the description of himself Stoker included, one such a 'keen physiognomist' as Whitman might desire?

> My friends call me Bram. I live at 43 Harcourt St., Dublin. I am a clerk in the service of the Crown on a small salary. I am twenty-four years old. Have been champion at our athletic sports (Trinity College, Dublin) and have won about a dozen cups. I have also been President of the College Philosophical Society and an art and theatrical critic of a daily paper. I am six feet two inches high and twelve stone weight naked and used to be forty-one or forty-two inches round the chest. I am ugly but strong and determined and have a large bump over my eyebrows. I have a heavy jaw and a big mouth and thick lips – sensitive nostrils – a snubnose and straight hair. I am equal in temper and cool in disposition and have a large amount of self control and am naturally secretive to the world. I take a delight in letting people I don't like – people of mean or cruel or sneaking or cowardly disposition – see the worst side of me. I have a large number of acquaintances and some five or six friends – all of which latter body care much for me. Now I have told you all I know about myself.

The novelist-to-be visited his hero the poet three times in the 1880s, when the theatrical company Stoker managed toured America. And although their conversations were summarized by Whitman's devoted amanuensis Horace Traubel, who would collect his observations in the nine volumes of his *Walt Whitman in Camden*, I still find myself wondering what they talked about.

Every atom belonging to me as good belongs to you.

I've always read Whitman's startling claim, at the beginning of his greatest poem, as a generous statement. But if Stoker indeed based his legend of appetite on the poet, then he turns this notion inside out: Every atom belonging to you is mine, your sweat, your tears, your lymphatic fluids, your semen if you're a man, your blood: I own you. That sentence in Kaplan's footnote shocks not because it's a stretch but because – despite the warmth we associate with Whitman and his legacy – it feels right somehow. I recognize him, the craving count, the barely bodied ancient thirst, inside the part of me that shares Whitman's love for the vital ember, the glowing health, the muscle and vigour of men. I wish I didn't. Every atom belonging to you: your semen, your blood. There he is in the mirror, shadow of the open-collared, slouch-hatted camerado.

INSATIABLE IS UNSUSTAINABLE: I'm in the parking lot at the natural foods store when the bumper sticker on the Toyota beside me stops me in my tracks. In context it's about consumption and the environment, clearly – we can't go on using more and more resources, producing and shopping and throwing things away, not if there's going to be a lasting human presence on this planet.

I get that, but what shakes me is that I'm reading the slogan in another, not entirely unrelated way. Because I have been insatiable – have forgotten, actually, what it might feel like to be satiated, or perhaps (it hurts to admit this) even to be satisfied. 'Satisfaction' is something I stopped seeking in sex, more or less, at least in a physical sense; what I wanted, in my long careening tour through the bodies of countless men, through bathhouse and sex club and online hook-ups and meth was something difficult to grasp. The rhetoric of addiction would describe it as an urge to flee my own sense of lack, seeking and seeking to disguise or ignore or fill an emptiness within – something like the way Carl Jung is supposed to have said to Bill W., 'You were reaching for spirit, you just reached for the wrong kind.' And indeed that's one way to view a deep, compelling attraction to bodies, a longing to touch and touch and enter.

I was 'partnered' – as postmodern parlance goes, or went, before same-sex marriage began to open different doors – to a man for sixteen years, and there was much pleasure and mutuality in our relation. And then there was, more clearly emergent over time, all that was left out, or wouldn't fit. I found this difficult to describe, this sense that not all of me could be expressed within our marriage. I began to use the metaphor of bandwidth, feeling even as I did so that it was partial, barely adequate.

If the self broadcasts on many channels, then Paul and I could clearly receive one another on, say, three of them, a nice mid-range. Because we were both writers and thus shared a social and professional world of considerable fascination, a mandarin realm we could discuss at length with few others, and because we liked domestic tranquillity and travel, and shared a deep pleasure in the work of description, trying to articulate what we saw – because of those things, we shared a mutual life. Outside of that: sex; adventure; the night; transgression; surprise; higher and lower pitches of experience. I need to be invited onto the back of a motorcycle and taken away now and then; I need a curtain pulled back, a hallway leading into some part of the world I've never seen. Paul feels that I have undervalued the mid-range, the welcome and comfort of the intimacy that arose from our long association. My friend Carol says that's what marriage is, there's no way around it. Still, I can't help but be hungry for the broader range of experience, the higher frequencies and the depths; I need, for whatever reasons, to live on that broader spectrum, or wither. I am coming to accept this about myself.

The ex-con in construction boots and a towel, smoking a hash pipe, flicking tiny coals and bits of ash from the down of his belly outdoors by the pool, the water-lights rippling over his torso.

The stoned, angelic young man, muscled and pale, opening his body to me and coaxing my fist inside him.

The oil worker who came in from days on the big oil rigs in the Gulf with his ears still ringing and his reddened skin hungry for touch.

The black man from the leather bar in Fresno who stood in front of me and came across my chest, then showed me a photo of his beautiful sixth-grade daughter and wept at how much he loved her.

The beautiful lean-muscled doctor – the first man I snorted crystal with – who whispered in my ear for hours about how he wanted me to infect him, covertly, without him knowing it, leaking virus into his bloodstream.

The landscaper who took me to his twenty-third-floor apartment, in a tower overlooking the park, and pissed on me on his terrace high above the lights of Houston while I lay on the concrete beneath him, entirely happy.

The bare-chested weightlifter in the gym, shorter than I was, thickly built, who stood behind me and guided my arms through a chest exercise as I pulled the cables taut in front of me and squeezed, and then pushed his chest into my back, and held me there, intently, without moving, so that I could feel his sweat and the pulse of his heart.

Men who wept about their fathers, their brothers, about bullies and gangs, about teachers and counsellors and coaches, but fathers most of all, those fountainheads of male woundings, because they sensed I was someone in whose presence they could set down their guard, or just someone willing to listen without judgement. A beautiful, compact hairy young bear from New Jersey – forty-something but nonetheless very young anyway – who shook in my arms, wearing just a clean white jockstrap, because no one had ever genuinely loved him. I didn't judge; it was as if that were part of my purpose: I wanted to know the men who moved through my nights like passing comets, wanted them to feel the pleasure of being known.

But do I want to describe myself as a sex addict? Doesn't a label like that sit on one like a tight suit, an ill-fitting little cage of identity that must of necessity leave out so many of the regions of the self? That's how I felt, sitting in a twelve-step meeting, talking with groups of fellow users of methamphetamine about the drug we had decided not to use: that we were collectively defining our identities by what we would not do, and that such an act of definition was a strange, subtle kind of self-murder. I understand that such a radical act might be necessary, in the face of an intractable self-destructiveness, to save one's life – but nonetheless I can't bring myself not to describe it as a kind of murder, because in any such act of self-definition (I'm Mark and I'm an addict) the other selves, some of whom are not named because they don't belong in this context, and some of whom aren't named because they cannot be, but remain phantoms, potentialities, shadows, little streams into the larger liquidity – well, all those aspects of oneself are more or less banished from the conversation, and they retreat a little further away, and then a little further again.

Addiction is one way to think about it. But Lacan says that all desire is based in a sense of lack. Once we experienced ourselves as whole, separated neither from the world nor from ourselves by language, but once a self and other is perceived, or something is objectified by being named, then we fall from Eden, and forever after we'll have the sense of something missing, of the irretrievable object – wholeness, oneself and the motherworld that bore us all of a piece. Therefore the veil is the figure of desire; if we tear it away, desire tends to disappear, but as soon as the veil is restored, the well of longing fills again.

Behind every man I want to kiss lies that original desire, which it is my nature and my fate to displace. Though displacement seems hardly the right word, if there is nothing else one can do.

When you have a lot of sex, sex becomes increasingly less narrative. There's less of a story of connection and its development, and more a series of images, like the list I've just written, a photo album of sorts, in which still pictures stand for a succession of bodies in time, in their beautiful or awkward arcs or spasms. Like Cavafy's poems, these remembered snapshots contained rooms of eros: a man who lay back in a sling in his darkened third-floor apartment, his shining red motorcycle spotlit beside him. Two identical tattooed men, tattooed rugby players, on their backs, side by side in a bare room in Seattle.

A long green hallway, in an East Village apartment, down which one had to move laterally, since there wasn't room to walk straight ahead, and at the end of it, a room entirely lined with, of all things, mid-century American pottery, arrayed on walls the sun had never touched.

A list, is that what desire makes, finally? As in so many of Whitman's poems, where line after line spins out a careening catalogue of what the poet sees, or is, or wishes to be. Ask the collector, the curator, the accumulator of sexual experience, the person who touches and touches what he desires: he is making, on paper or in his head or in his dream-life, a list.

To an American like Whitman (though there is no American like him, the progenitor of our hopes for ourselves too secret to quite name, the originator of the notion that democracy might be founded in the body, on the affection between bodies), elation in the face of the vital must have seemed an exhilarating rejection of the puritan heritage of division between body and soul. Was anyone ever so sanguine about sex? Blake, maybe, whose work Whitman read, though at what point in his career we don't quite know.

But to a European, perhaps this uprush of energy in the face of the body and its vital fluids had perhaps another cast altogether. For Stoker, it may have seemed that what was wan or dead in the self might be refreshed temporarily and, finally, horrifyingly, by the hot juices of those who were more immediately alive. Is vampirism a matter of the overly self-conscious being awakened to life by the vitality of those who are barely self-conscious at all? Is that why Whitman liked stevedores and streetcar conductors and Long Island baymen, the big guys at home in their bodies, who would never think to write a poem?

Or let's say Stoker, who married a woman Oscar Wilde had proposed to before Bram came along, found it necessary to suppress his own desires, to the degree that he would project them out onto a horrifying sub-human or post-human creature, who has no firm foundation in biology, but must feed off the juices of others, without choice or sunlight. And in doing so, perhaps he reversed the gestures of his old idol. Where Whitman had written his beautiful poem of the sexual union between body and soul:

> I mind how once we lay, such a transparent summer
>   morning,
> How you settled your head athwart my hips, and gently
>   turned over upon me,
> And parted the shirt from my bosom-bone, and plunged
>   your tongue to my bare-stript heart,
> And reached till you felt my beard, and reached till you held
>   my feet.

Stoker has offered us a parallel physical situation with an entirely inverted tone:

> . . . he pulled open his shirt, and with his long sharp nails
> opened a vein in his breast. When the blood began to spurt out,
> he took my hands in one of his, holding them tight, and with
> the other seized my neck and pressed my mouth to the wound,
> so that I must either suffocate or swallow.

W hitman fuses the erotic and the spiritual, as the kiss to the bare chest begins an epiphanic experience, a moment of peace and of understanding, whereas the mouth is brought to Dracula's chest in a kind of rape, a horrible force-feeding which can lead only to repulsion and contagion.

And so there it is: the intersection of the chosen and the compulsive, of consuming and being consumed, of the celebratory and of erasure.

A ddiction is one way to think about it. But there's also what seems to have been Whitman's view – a mission, if you will, to seek out one's cameradoes, to join in the community of lovers, bound together by desire and affection, to find the common good in our common skin. This vision comes most clear in the Calamus poems, and in parts of 'Song of Myself'. It is primarily an imaginative union among men; Whitman's women, unfortunately, seem either afterthoughts or engines of procreation. He comes close to granting them freely moving sexual desires, and a position as democratic citizens, but he cannot really seem to desire them, and thus they are excluded from the essential bond – eros – that holds his cameradoes together in the new democratic union.

There are lists of men in Whitman's papers, with brief notations – an age, a bit of detail, a note about how they met. Not much. A collector's catalogue, a record of the body's travels? How else will I know the world, if not by touching as much of it as possible, finding in the bodies of my lovers and fellows my coordinates?

O r there's Teilhard de Chardin, brilliant radical Catholic, palaeontologist and physicist, who refashions the poet's claim on our shared atoms this way: 'However narrowly the heart of an atom may be circumscribed,' he writes, 'its realm is co-extensive, at least potentially, with that of every other atom.' We are all co-extensive, and our work is to move toward union; evolution, de Chardin posits, is a collective motion toward greater consciousness. 'No evolutionary future,' he writes in *The Phenomenon of Man*, 'awaits anyone except in association with everyone else.' We must know our fellows in order for everything to move forward; it is our spiritual imperative to connect, or else the destiny of the world cannot be completed.

A theory of the popularity of vampire books and movies: we understand that in a consumer culture we are feasting on whatever brings us a feeling of life, that we hunger to be fed in this way, that our freedom to act upon our desires places us in the position of hungry consumers, seeking the next pleasure.

Buy anything and what you've brought into your life has made the world a little less vital someplace else.

And we consume our lovers, of course, as we know the world by mouth.

'By mouth' means to use our lips and tongues to touch, but also to speak, to name.

To consume as in tasting. Or as in absorbing, taking on their characteristics or vital energy.

Historians disagree about Whitman's sexual life; some suggest that he had actual congress with few, or none. I doubt that very much, though the evidence for my claim is based on feeling, on the rich and tender erotic force of the poetry, which seems to me composed out of the knowledge of skin. I would like to think he touched men, as he would say 'long and long', and I would like to believe – of him and of myself – that this deep and attentive touching was a necessary sort of research, that his poems could not have come swimming into being from any other source but physical love, which he did not distinguish from the spiritual kind.

Great poets are, by definition, undead. The voice is preserved in the warm saline of ink and of memory. It cannot fade; time cannot take away a word of it. The personality, as it breathes through the preserved voice back into the world, is unmistakable: Walt Whitman sounds like no one else. And of all poets, he seems to have understood in the most uncanny of ways that his audience did not yet exist.

He was creating it, in his poems, summoning readers into being who could receive what he had to say. This is most clearly stated in 'Crossing Brooklyn Ferry', a poem that has never failed to make me shiver, though I have read it countless times. Where is the speaker in the poem? On the ferry where in a few years the Brooklyn Bridge will stand, yes, in his own time, but also strangely present in our moment:

> It avails not, neither time or place – distance avails not,
> I am with you, you men and women of a generation,
>   or ever so many generations hence,
> I project myself – also I return – I am with you, and know
>   how it is.

Later in the poem, he returns to this sort of performative speech, willing himself outside of time – or is it further into it? – approaching his readers in their present moment, as if pushing upward through the skin of the page itself:

> Closer yet I approach you,
> What thought you have of me, I had as much of you – I laid
>   in my stores in advance,
> I considered long and seriously of you before you were born.
>
> Who was to know what should come home to me?
> Who knows but I am enjoying this?
> Who knows but I am as good as looking at you now, for all
>   you cannot see me?

There is perhaps one other poem like this in English, a fragment by John Keats that begins: 'This living hand . . .' Who else would dare to speak this way, to write themselves into the condition of deathlessness?

Of the many poems that demonstrate Whitman's daring, 'Trickle, Drops' is in its way the strangest. He placed it in the yearning, homoerotic Calamus sequence, for good reason, and I used to think it the creepiest page in *Leaves of Grass*. But in the light of Stoker, I begin to see it differently indeed, though I admit it still makes my skin crawl a little. Who's the vampire here?

> O drops of me! trickle, slow drops,
> Candid, from me falling – drip, bleeding drops,
> From wounds made to free you whence you were prisoned,
> From my face – from my forehead and lips,
> From my breast – from within where I was concealed –
>   Press forth, red drops – confession drops,
> Stain every page – stain every song I sing, every word I say,
>   bloody drops,
> Let them know your scarlet heat – let them glisten,
> Saturate them with yourself, all ashamed and wet,
> Glow upon all I have written or shall write, bleeding drops,
> Let it all be seen in your light, blushing drops.

With his characteristic, canny strangeness, Whitman has done what no one else would have thought to do. He's made the reader the vampire, feasting on the poems, which here expose, in their fierce confessional heat, the poet's naked life. And where 'you', Whitman's ubiquitous second person, is nearly everywhere in his work, the reader he wishes to seduce and to claim, here he speaks, for once, to his own blood. He feeds it to us. I feel – as indeed he must have wanted his readers to feel – that he feeds it to me. How could I refuse him? ■

GRANTA

THE
COLONEL'S SON

Roberto Bolaño

TRANSLATED FROM THE SPANISH BY CHRIS ANDREWS

You're not going to believe this, but last night, at about 4 a.m., I saw a movie on TV that could have been my biography or my autobiography or a summary of my days on this bitch of a planet. It scared me so fucking shitless I tell you I just about fell off my chair.

I could tell straight away it was a bad film, or the sort we call bad – poor fools that we are – because the actors aren't much good and the director's not much good and the cretinous special-effects guys are pretty hopeless too. But really it was just a very low-budget film, pure B-grade schlock. What I mean, just to be perfectly clear, is a film that cost about four euros or five dollars. I don't know who had to get laid to raise the money, but I can tell you that all the producer shelled out was a bit of small change, and they had to make do with that.

I can't even remember the title, really I can't, but I'll go to my grave calling it *The Colonel's Son*, and I swear it was the most democratic, the most revolutionary film I'd seen in ages, and I don't say that because the film in itself revolutionized anything; not at all, it was pathetic really, full of clichés and tired devices, prejudices and stereotypes, and yet at the same time, every frame was infused with and gave off a revolutionary atmosphere, or rather an atmosphere in which you could sense the revolution, not in its totality, but a fragment, a microscopic fragment of the revolution, as if you were watching *Jurassic Park*, except the dinosaurs never showed, no, I mean as if it was *Jurassic Park* and no one ever even *mentioned* the fucking reptiles, but their presence was inescapable and unbearably oppressive.

Do you see what I'm getting at? I've never read any of Osvaldo

Lamborghini's *Proletarian Chamber Theatre*, but I'm certain that Lamborghini, with his masochistic streak, would have been happy to watch *The Colonel's Son* at three or four in the morning.

What was the film about? Well, don't laugh; it was about zombies. But if the political background to George Romero's films is Karl Marx, the political background to the film last night was Arthur Rimbaud and Alfred Jarry. Pure French insanity.

Don't laugh. Romero is straightforward and tragic: he talks about communities sinking into the mire and about survivors. He also has a sense of humour. You remember his second film, the one where the zombies wander around the mall because that's the only place they can vaguely remember from their previous lives? Well, last night's film was different. It didn't have much of a sense of humour, although I laughed like a madman, and it wasn't about a communal tragedy either. The protagonist was a boy who – I'm guessing, because I didn't see the start – turns up one day with his girlfriend at the place where his father works. I didn't see the start, like I said, so I can't be sure. Maybe the boy goes to visit his father and that's where he meets the girl. Her name is Julie and she's pretty and young, and she wants to be – or seem to be – up to date, the way young people do. The boy is the son of Colonel Reynolds. The colonel is a widower and loves his son – that's obvious right from the start – but he's also a soldier, so the relationship that he has with his son is one in which there's no place for displays of affection.

What is Julie doing at the base? We don't know. Maybe she went to deliver some pizzas and got lost. Maybe she's the sister of one of the guinea pigs that Colonel Reynolds is using, although that seems unlikely. Maybe she met the colonel's son when she was hitching a ride out of the city. What we do know is that Julie is there and that at some point she gets lost in an underground labyrinth and innocently walks through a door that she never should have opened. On the other side is a zombie, and it starts chasing her. Julie flees, of course, but the zombie manages to corner her and scratch her; at one point he even bites her arm and her legs. The scene is suggestive of a rape.

Then the colonel's son, who has been searching for her, appears, and between them they manage to overpower and kill the zombie, if such a thing is possible. Then they race down increasingly narrow and tortuous underground passages, until they finally make their way out through the sewers to the surface. As they're escaping, Julie begins to feel the first symptoms of the illness. She is tired and hungry and begs the colonel's son to leave her or forget her. His resolve, however, is inexhaustible. He has fallen in love with Julie, or perhaps he was already in love (which suggests that he has known her for some time); in any case, armed with the generosity of the very young, he has no intention, come what may, of leaving her to face her fate alone.

When they reach the surface, Julie's hunger is uncontrollable. The streets have a desolate look. The film was probably shot on the outskirts of some North American city: deserted neighbourhoods, half-derelict buildings that directors who have no budget use for shooting after midnight; so that's where they end up, the colonel's son and Julie, who's hungry and has been complaining all the time they were running away. It hurts, I'm hungry, but the colonel's son doesn't seem to hear; all he cares about is saving Julie, getting away from the military base and never seeing his father again.

The relationship between father and son is odd. It's clear from the start that the colonel puts his son before his duties as a soldier, but of course his love isn't reciprocated; the son has a long way to go before he'll be able to understand his father, or solitude, or the sad fate to which all beings are condemned. Young Reynolds is, after all, an adolescent, and he's in love and nothing else matters to him. But careful, don't be misled by appearances. The son appears to be a young fool, a young hothead, rash and thoughtless, just like we were, except that he speaks English, and his particular desert is a devastated neighbourhood in a North American megalopolis, while we speak Spanish (or something similar) and live and stifle on desolate avenues in the cities of Latin America.

When the pair emerges from the maze of underground passages, the landscape is somehow familiar to us. The lighting is poor; the windows of the buildings are smashed; there are hardly any cars on the streets.

The colonel's son drags Julie to a food store. One of those stores that stays open till three or four in the morning. A filthy store where tins of food are stacked up next to chocolate bars and bags of potato chips. There's only one guy working there. Naturally, he's an immigrant, and to judge from his age and the look of anxiety and annoyance that comes over his face, he must be the owner. The colonel's son leads Julie to the counter where the doughnuts and the sweets are, but Julie goes straight to the fridge and starts eating a raw hamburger. The storekeeper is watching them through the one-way mirror, and when he sees her throw up he comes out and asks if they're trying to eat without paying. The colonel's son reaches into the pocket of his jeans and throws him some bills.

At this point, four people come in. They're Mexicans. It's not hard to imagine them taking classes at a drama school, or, for that matter, dealing drugs on the corners of their neighbourhood, or picking tomatoes with John Steinbeck's farmhands. Three guys and a girl, in their twenties, mindless and ready to die in any old alleyway. The Mexicans show an interest in Julie's vomit too. The storekeeper says the money's not enough. The colonel's son says it is. Who's going to pay for the damage? Who's going to pay for this filth? says the storekeeper, pointing at the vomit, which is a nuclear shade of green. While they're arguing, one of the Mexicans has slipped in behind the till and is emptying it. Meanwhile, the other three are staring at the vomit as if it conceals the secret of the universe.

When the storekeeper realizes he's being robbed, he pulls out a pistol and threatens the Mexicans. This gives the colonel's son a chance to grab a few sweets from the counter and beg Julie to get out of there with him, but Julie has gone back to the raw meat, and as she tears into a steak, she begins to cry and says she doesn't understand and implores young Reynolds to do something. The Mexicans start brawling with the storekeeper. They pull out their knives and flash them in the bluish light of the food store. They manage to get hold of the storekeeper's pistol and shoot him. He drops to the floor. One of the Mexicans goes to the counter where the alcoholic drinks are kept and grabs some bottles without bothering to see what kind of liquor they contain. As he passes Julie, she bites him on the arm. The Mexican howls. Julie sinks her teeth in and won't let go, despite the pleas of the colonel's son. Another gunshot.

Someone shouts, C'mon, let's go. The Mexican manages to pull his arm free and catches up with his companions, crying out in pain. Young Reynolds examines the storekeeper's body lying on the floor. He's alive, he says. We have to get him to a hospital. No, says Julie, leave him, the police will take care of him. Their steps, as they walk out of the store, are quick but unsteady. They see a black van parked outside and break into it. Just as young Reynolds manages to get it going, the storekeeper appears and begs them to take him to a hospital. Julie looks at the man but doesn't say a word. The storekeeper's white shirt is stained with blood. The colonel's son tells him to get in. When he's in the van and they're about to go, they hear the siren of a police car. Then the storekeeper says he wants to get out. Can't do that, says the colonel's son, and tears away.

The chase begins. It doesn't take long for the police to start shooting. The storekeeper opens the van's back door and shouts, That's enough. He's cut down by a hail of bullets. Julie, who's sitting in the back seat, turns and peers into the darkness. She hears him crying. The storekeeper is crying for the life that's slipping away from him, a life of ceaseless work and struggling in a foreign land to give his family a better future. And now it's all over.

Then Julie gets out of her seat and goes into the back part of the van. And while the colonel's son shakes off the police, Julie starts eating the storekeeper's chest. With a radiant smile on his face, Reynolds turns to Julie and says, We've lost the cops, but she is crouched on all fours in the back, as if she were a tiger or were making love, and her only reaction is to breathe a satisfied sigh, because she's assuaged her appetite; momentarily, as we shall soon discover. All the colonel's son can do, of course, is cry out in terror. Then he says,

What have you done, Julie? How could you do that? It's clear from his tone of voice, however, that he's in love, and that although his girl is a cannibal, she is still, above all, his girl. Julie's reply is simple: she was hungry.

At this point, while young Reynolds is mutely venting his exasperation, the police car appears again and the young pair resumes their flight through dark, deserted streets. There's still a surprise in store for us: when the police open fire on the fugitives, the back door of the van opens, and the storekeeper appears, but he's become a ravenous zombie. First he tears open a cop's throat, then sets on the guy's partner, who empties the magazine of his gun at him, in vain, then freezes in horror, before being devoured in turn. Just then, two cars from the military base close off the alley, and using two rather strange weapons, like laser guns, neutralize first the storekeeper and then the two zombie policemen. Colonel Reynolds gets out of one of the cars and asks his soldiers if they've seen his son. The soldiers reply in the negative. Another car appears in the alley and a woman, Colonel Landovski, gets out. She informs Reynolds that from now on, she'll be in charge of the operation. Reynolds says he doesn't give a damn who's in charge, all he wants is to find his son safe and sound. Your son's probably been infected by now, says Colonel Landovski. It's an odd scene: Landovski takes on the role of 'father', prepared to sacrifice the boy, while Reynolds takes on the role of 'mother', prepared to do anything to ensure the survival of his son.

A fifth or sixth car pulls up at the corner, but no one gets out. It belongs to the Mexicans. They recognize the van from the food store, the van in which the young lovers fled. One of the Mexicans, the one Julie bit, is pretty sick. He's running a fever and raving incoherently. He wants to eat. I'm hungry, he keeps telling his friends. He asks them to take him to a hospital. The Mexican girl backs him up on that. We have to take him to a hospital, she says sensibly. The other two agree, but first they want to find the bitch who bit Chucho and teach her a lesson she'll never forget.

Since we forget everything in the end, I'm only guessing that they're talking about killing her. They spur each other on to vengeance. They speak of honour, respect, decency, the things they believe in. Then they start the car and drive off. At no point do the soldiers show any sign of having noticed them, as if this ghostly street were a busy thoroughfare.

In the following scene, Julie and young Reynolds are walking over a bridge. Where can we find a taxi? the boy wonders. Julie announces that she can't walk any further. On the other side of the bridge is a phone booth. Wait for me here, says young Reynolds, and runs off towards the booth, only to find that there's no directory and that the receiver has been ripped out. Looking back, he sees that Julie has climbed onto the balustrade of the bridge. He shouts, Julie, don't! and starts running. But Julie jumps and her body disappears into the water, although it soon floats to the surface and is swept away by the current, face down. The colonel's son goes down a stairway to the river. The water is very shallow: thirty centimetres, a metre at the deepest. The river has man-made banks and even the bed has been paved. A homeless black man, hidden among some concrete pillars down the river, is watching young Reynolds. The boy's search brings him to the black guy, who tells him to give up, the girl is dead. No, says the colonel's son, and goes on searching, closely followed by the black guy.

When young Reynolds finds her, the girl is floating in a pool. Julie, Julie, calls her young lover, and the girl, who has been face down in the water for who knows how many minutes, coughs and calls his name. I've never seen anything like it all my fucking life, says the black guy.

Just then, the Mexicans appear (the verb *to appear* will appear often in this story), fifty metres away. They've got out of their car and are looking on; one is sitting on the bonnet, another leaning against a mudguard and the girl is up on the roof; only the wounded guy is still inside, watching or trying to watch them through the window. The Mexicans make menacing gestures and threaten them with a litany of punishments, tortures and humiliations. This is getting nasty, says the black guy. Follow me. They enter the city's system of sewers. The Mexicans follow them. But the labyrinth of tunnels is sufficiently complicated for the black guy and the young couple to lose their pursuers. Finally they reach a refuge that's almost as welcoming as a nightclub. This is my place, says the black guy. Then he tells them the story of his life. The jobs he's had to do. The constant presence of the police. The hardbitten life of a North American working man in the twentieth or twenty-first century. My muscles couldn't take any more, says the black guy.

His place isn't bad. He has a bed, where they lay Julie down, and books, which, so he says, he has picked up over the years in the sewers. Self-help books and books about the revolution and books on technical subjects, like how to repair a lawnmower. There's also a kind of bathroom, with a primitive shower. This water's always clean, says the black guy. A stream of crystal-clear water falls continually from a hole in the ceiling. We all build our shelters from whatever we can find, he explains. Then he picks up an iron bar and says that they can rest; he'll go out and keep watch.

It's always night in the sewers, but that night, the last night of peace, is particularly strange. The boy falls asleep in a shabby armchair after making love with Julie. The black guy falls asleep too, mumbling incomprehensibly. The girl is the only one who doesn't feel sleepy, and she goes into other rooms, because her appetite has begun to rage again. But with a difference: now Julie knows that self-inflicted pain can be a substitute for food. So we see her sticking needles in her face and piercing her nipples with wires.

At this point the Mexicans reappear and easily overpower first the black guy, then the son of Colonel Reynolds. They look for the girl. They shout threats. If she doesn't come out of her hiding place, they'll kill the black guy and her boyfriend. Then a door opens and Julie appears. She has changed a lot. She has become the indisputable queen of piercing. The leader of the Mexicans (the biggest guy) finds her attractive. The sick Mexican is lying on the ground, begging them to take him to a hospital. The Mexican girl is comforting him, but her eyes are fixed on the new Julie. The other Mexican is holding the colonel's son, who is screaming like a man possessed; the possibility (or the strong probability) that Julie will be raped is more than he can bear. The black guy is lying unconscious on the ground.

Julie and the Mexican shut themselves in a room. No, Julie, no, no, no, sobs young Reynolds. The Mexican's voice can be heard through the door: That's it, baby. C'mon, let's get that off. Holy shit! You really do like those hooks, don't you? Kneel down baby, yeah, that's it, that's it. Lift up your ass, perfect, oh yeah. And more stuff like that until suddenly he starts yelling, and there are blows, as if someone was getting kicked, or thrown against a wall, then picked up and thrown against the opposite wall, and then the yelling stops and there's only the sound of biting and chewing, until the door opens and Julie appears again with her lips (the whole of her face, actually) smeared with blood, holding the Mexican's head in one hand.

Which makes the other Mexican crazy; he pulls out a pistol, goes up and empties it into the girl, but of course the bullets don't harm her at all, and Julie laughs contentedly before grabbing the guy's shirt, pulling him towards her and tearing his throat open with a single bite. Young Reynolds and the black guy, who has recovered consciousness, are gaping at the scene. The Mexican girl, however, has the presence of mind to try to escape, but Julie catches her as she's climbing a metal stairway that leads to the mouth of the upper sewer. The girl kicks and pours out insults, but then, yielding to Julie's greater strength, she lets go and falls. Don't do it, Julie, the colonel's son has just enough time to say, before his sweetheart's teeth destroy the face of the Mexican girl. Then Julie extracts her victim's heart and eats it.

At this point, a voice says: So you think you've won, you whore? Julie turns around and what we see is the last Mexican, now fully transformed into a zombie. The two of them begin to fight. Julie is helped by the black guy and her boyfriend and for a few seconds it looks like she's going to win. But Julie's victims pick themselves up and join in the fight, and zombies, it seems, are ten times stronger than normal humans, which means that the fight inevitably begins to go the Mexicans' way. So our three heroes flee. The black guy takes them to a room. They barricade the door. The black guy tells them to go; he'll try, God knows how, to stop the zombies. Julie and young Reynolds don't have to be told twice, and go off to another room. At one point in their flight, Julie looks her boyfriend in the eye and asks him, just with her gaze or maybe with words, I can't remember now, how he can still love her. Young Reynolds replies by kissing her on the cheek, then he wipes his lips and kisses her on the mouth. I love you, he says, I love you more than ever.

Then they hear a yell and they know that the black guy is gone. There's no way out of the room where they've taken refuge; it's full of old furniture piled up chaotically, but with passages between; it's like a labyrinth of the transient, of things without the will to last. I have to leave you, says Julie. Young Reynolds doesn't know what she means. Only when Julie uses her extraordinary strength to throw him under some armchairs and broken-down washing machines and faulty or obsolete television sets does he understand that the girl is prepared to sacrifice herself for him. He hardly has time to react. Julie goes out and fights and loses and the Mexican zombies are coming for him. With tears streaming down his face, young Reynolds tries to make himself invisible, curling up into a ball of flesh under the pile of junk.

The Mexican zombies, however, find him and try to drag him out of there. Young Reynolds sees their hungry faces, then the hungry face of the black guy and Julie's face, watching him, showing no sign of emotion. At this point, Colonel Reynolds, escorted by three of his men, kicks down the door and starts blowing away all the zombies with the special gun. All the time he's firing, the colonel is calling his son's name. Here I am, Dad, says young Reynolds.

The nightmare is over.

The next scene shows the colonel comfortably seated in his office proposing to his son that they go to Alaska for a vacation together. Young Reynolds says he'll think it over. There's no rush, son, says the colonel. Then the colonel's on his own and he begins to smile, as if he can't quite believe how incredibly lucky he's been. His son is alive.

THE COLONEL'S SON

Meanwhile, young Reynolds has left his father's office and started walking through the underground passageways at the base. There's a look of deep uneasiness on his face. Gradually, distant noises begin to penetrate his self-absorption. He can hear shouts and howls, the cries of people for whom pain has become a way of life. Without being able to stop himself, he starts walking towards the source of the cries. He doesn't have to go far. The passage turns a corner and there is a door; it opens onto an enormous laboratory, stretching away before him.

He is warmly greeted by some military scientists who have known him since he was a boy. He continues on his way. He discovers a series of glass cells. The Mexicans have been placed in them, each in a separate cell. He keeps walking. He finds Julie's cell. Julie recognizes him. The colonel's son puts his hand on the glass and Julie puts her hand up to his, as if she were touching it. In a larger cell some scientists are working on the black guy. He could become a great warrior, they say. They are sending electric shocks through his brain. The black guy is full of hatred and resentment. He howls. The colonel's son hides in a corner. When the scientists go for their coffee break, he gets up and asks the black guy if he recognizes him. Vaguely, says the black guy. All my memories are vague. And fucking strange, too.

We were friends, says the colonel's son. We met by the river. I remember an apartment on 30th Street, says the black guy, and a woman laughing, but I don't know what I was doing there. The boy frees the black guy from his chains. Freed, he walks like a kind of robocop. A zombie robocop. Don't attack me, says the colonel's son, I'm your friend. I understand, says the black guy, who goes to a shelf and takes down an assault rifle. When the scientists come back, the black guy greets them with a volley of fire. Meanwhile, the boy frees Julie and tells her that they have to flee again. They kiss. The soldiers try to take out the black guy. As Julie and her boyfriend are sneaking away, she frees the Mexicans. More soldiers arrive. The bullets destroy some containers where body parts are kept. Viscera and spinal columns crawl over the floor of the laboratory. A siren begins to shriek. In this pitched battle it isn't clear which side has the advantage, or even if there really are sides, not just individuals fighting for their own lives and for the deaths of the others. Over the PA a voice is repeating: Block the passages on level five. My son! shouts Colonel Reynolds and rushes down to level five like a madman.

Colonel Landovski shoots the black guy to bits and is devoured in turn by the Mexican girl. The soldiers repel an attack mounted by bloody pieces of human flesh. The second attack, however, breaks through their lines of defence and they're devoured by tiny scraps of raw meat. There are more and more zombies. The battle becomes totally chaotic. The colonel reaches level five. Through a window he sees his son and Julie, and gestures to show that the passage is still open, there is still an escape route. The colonel's son takes Julie by the hand and they head in the direction that his father indicated. I'm hurting all over, says Julie. Don't start that again, says the boy. When we get away from here you'll feel better. Do you believe me? I believe you, says Julie.

In the passage that hasn't yet been blocked, Colonel Reynolds appears, unarmed, his shirt drenched with sweat, not only because he has hasn't stopped running but also because the temperature on level five has increased dramatically. Colonel Reynolds's face has been transfigured. It could be said that his expression resembles that of Abraham. With every cell in his body he calls out his son's name and repeats how dearly he loves him. His military career, his scientific research, duty, honour and his country are all swept away by the force of love. Here, through here. Follow me. Hurry up. Soon the doors will shut automatically. Come with me and you'll be able to escape. All he gets in response is the sad gaze of his son, who at this moment, and perhaps for the first time, *knows* more than his father. The father at one end of the passage. The son at the other end. And suddenly the doors shut and they're separated forever.

Behind the son there's a kind of furnace. It isn't clear whether the furnace was there already or whether the fire caused by the zombie rebellion has spread. It's some blaze. Julie and the boy hold hands. Come on, Julie, says the boy, don't be afraid, nothing will separate us now. Meanwhile, on the other side, the colonel is trying to break down the door, in vain. The young couple walk towards the fire and disappear. The screen goes an intense red. The only sound is a machine gun hammering. Then an explosion, screams, groans, electrical sparking. On the other side, shut off from all this, the colonel is still trying to break down the door. ∎

GRANTA

'A timely anthology of short stories [that] reveals the strength of
contemporary African fiction' – *Prospect*

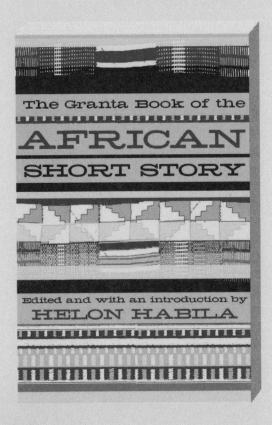

Twenty-nine short stories selected and introduced by
one of Africa's most eminent contemporary writers.
A showcase of the best in African fiction.

GRANTABOOKS.COM

Give the gift
of new writing

'Provides enough to satisfy the most rabid appetite for good writing and hard thinking' – *Washington Post*

Buy a gift subscription to *Granta*
and save over 40% off the cover price

US
$45.99

CANADA
$57.99

LATIN AMERICA
$65.99

Subscribe now by completing the form overleaf,
visiting granta.com or calling toll free 1-866-438-6150

GRANTA.COM

GRANTA

THE MAGAZINE OF NEW WRITING

SUBSCRIPTION FORM FOR USA, CANADA AND LATIN AMERICA

Yes, I would like to take out a subscription to *Granta*.

GUARANTEE: If I am ever dissatisfied with my *Granta* subscription, I will simply notify you, and you will send me a complete refund or credit my credit card, as applicable, for all un-mailed issues.

YOUR DETAILS   GIFT RECIPIENT DETAILS

MR / MISS / MRS / DR ....   MR / MISS / MRS / DR ....
NAME ....   NAME ....
ADDRESS ....   ADDRESS ....
....
CITY............................... STATE ....   CITY............................... STATE ....
ZIP CODE .... COUNTRY ....   ZIP CODE .... COUNTRY ....
EMAIL ....   EMAIL ....
(Only provide your email if you are happy for Granta to communicate with you this way)

☐ Please check this box if you do not wish to receive special offers from *Granta*
☐ Please check this box if you do not wish to receive offers from organizations selected by *Granta*

YOUR PAYMENT DETAILS

1 year subscription: ☐USA: $45.99 ☐Canada: $57.99 ☐Latin America: $65.99

3 year subscription: ☐USA: $112.50 ☐Canada: $148.50 ☐Latin America: $172.50

Enclosed is my check for $_____ made payable to *Granta*.

Please charge my: ☐Visa ☐Mastercard ☐Amex

Card No. ☐☐☐☐☐☐☐☐☐☐☐☐☐☐☐☐

Exp. ☐☐☐☐

Security Code ☐☐☐☐

SIGNATURE ....   DATE ....

Please mail this order form with your payment instructions to:

Granta Publications
PO Box 359
Congers NY 10920-0359

Or call toll free 1-866-438-6150
Or visit GRANTA.COM for details

Source code: BUS117PM

GRANTA

THE DUNE

Stephen King

A s the Judge climbs into the kayak beneath a bright morning sky, a slow and clumsy process that takes him almost five minutes, he reflects that an old man's body is nothing but a sack filled with aches and indignities. Eighty years ago, when he was ten, he jumped into a wooden canoe and cast off, with no bulky life jacket, no worries, and certainly with no pee dribbling into his underwear. Every trip out to the little unnamed island began with a great and uneasy excitement. Now there is only unease. And pain that seems centred deep in his guts and radiates everywhere. But he still makes the trip. Many things have lost their allure in these shadowy later years – most things, really – but not the dune on the far side of the island. Never the dune.

In the early days of his exploration, he expected the dune to be gone after every big storm, and following the 1944 hurricane that sank the USS *Raleigh* off Siesta Key, he was sure it would be. But when the skies cleared, the island was still there. So was the dune, although the hundred-mile-an-hour winds should have blown all the sand away, leaving only the bare rocks. Over the years he has debated back and forth about whether the magic is in him or in the dune. Perhaps it's both, but surely most of it is in the dune.

Since 1932, he has crossed this short stretch of water thousands of times. Usually there's nothing but rocks and bushes and sand; sometimes there is something else.

Settled in the kayak at last, he paddles slowly from the beach to the island, his frizz of white hair blowing around his mostly bald skull. A few turkey buzzards wheel overhead, making their ugly conversation. Once he was the son of the richest man on the Florida Gulf coast, then he was a lawyer, then he was a judge on the Pinellas County

Circuit, then he was appointed to the State Supreme Court. There was talk, during the Reagan years, of a nomination to the United States Supreme Court, but that never happened, and a week after the idiot Clinton became president, Judge Harvey Beecher – just Judge to his many acquaintances (he has no real friends) in Sarasota, Osprey, Nokomis and Venice – retired. Hell, he never liked Tallahassee, anyway. It's cold up there.

Also, it's too far from the island, and its peculiar dune. On these early-morning kayak trips, paddling the short distance on smooth water, he's willing to admit that he's addicted to it. But who wouldn't be addicted to a thing like this?

On the rocky east side, a gnarled bush juts from the split in a guano-splattered rock. This is where he ties up, and he's always careful with the knot. It wouldn't do to be stranded out here. His father's estate (that's how he still thinks of it, although the elder Beecher has been gone for forty years now) covers almost two miles of prime Gulf-front property, the main house is far inland, on the Sarasota Bay side, and there would be no one to hear him yelling. Tommy Curtis, the caretaker, might notice him gone and come looking; more likely, he would just assume the Judge was locked up in his study, where he often spends whole days, supposedly working on his memoirs.

Once upon a time Mrs Riley might have become nervous if he didn't come out of the study for lunch, but now he hardly ever eats at noon (she calls him 'nothing but a stuffed string', but never to his face). There's no other staff, and both Curtis and Riley know he can be cross when he's interrupted. Not that there's really much to interrupt; he hasn't added so much as a line to the memoirs in two years, and in his heart he knows they will never be finished. The unfinished recollections of a Florida judge? No great loss there. The one story he *could* write is the one he never will. The Judge wants no talk at his funeral about how, in his last years, a previously fine intellect was corrupted by senility.

He's even slower getting out of the kayak than he was getting in, and turns turtle once, wetting his shirt and trousers in the little waves that run up the gravelly shingle. Beecher is not discommoded. It isn't the first time he's fallen, and there's no one to see him. He supposes it's unwise to continue these trips at his age, even though the island is so close to the mainland, but stopping isn't an option. An addict is an addict is an addict.

Beecher struggles to his feet and clutches his belly until the last of the pain subsides. He brushes sand and shells from his trousers, double-checks his mooring rope, then spots one of the turkey buzzards perched on the island's largest rock, peering down at him.

'Hi!' he shouts in the voice he now hates – cracked and wavering, the voice of a fishwife. 'Hi, you bugger! Get on about your business.'

After a brief rustle of its raggedy wings, the turkey buzzard sits right where it is. Its beady eyes seem to say, *But, Judge – today you* are *my business.*

Beecher stoops, picks up a larger shell and shies it at the bird. This time it does fly away, the sound of its wings like rippling cloth. It soars across the short stretch of water and lands on his dock. *Still,* the Judge thinks, *a bad omen.* He remembers a fellow on the Florida State Patrol telling him once that turkey buzzards didn't just know where carrion was; they also knew where carrion *would be.*

'I can't tell you,' the patrolman said, 'how many times I've seen those ugly bastards circling a spot on the Tamiami where there's a fatal wreck a day or two later. Sounds crazy, I know, but just about any Florida road cop will tell you the same.'

There are almost always turkey buzzards out here on the little no-name island. He supposes it smells like death to them, and why not? What else?

The Judge sets off on the little path he has beaten over the years. He will check the dune on the other side, where the sand is beach-fine instead of stony and shelly, and then he will return to the kayak and drink his little jug of cold tea. He may doze awhile in the morning sun (he dozes often these days, supposes most nonagenarians do), and when he wakes (*if* he wakes), he'll make the return trip. He tells himself that the dune will be just a smooth blank upslope of sand, as it is most days, but he knows better.

That damned buzzard knew better, too.

He spends a long time on the sandy side, with his age-warped fingers clasped in a knot behind him. His back aches, his shoulders ache, his hips ache, his knees ache; most of all, his gut aches. But he pays these things no mind. Perhaps later, but not now.

He looks at the dune, and what is written there.

A nthony Wayland arrives at Beecher's Pelican Point estate bang on 7 p.m., just as promised. One thing the Judge has always appreciated – both in the courtroom and out of it – is punctuality, and the boy is punctual. He reminds himself never to call Wayland *boy* to his face (although, this being the South, *son* is OK). Wayland wouldn't understand that, when you're ninety, any fellow under the age of forty looks like a boy.

'Thank you for coming,' the Judge says, ushering Wayland into his study. It's just the two of them; Curtis and Mrs Riley have long since gone to their homes in Nokomis Village. 'You brought the necessary document?'

'Yes, indeed, Judge,' Wayland says. He opens his attorney's briefcase and removes a thick document bound by a large steel clip. The pages aren't vellum, as they would have been in the old days, but they are rich and heavy just the same. At the top of the first, in forbidding Gothic type (what the Judge has always thought of as graveyard type), are the words Last Will and Testament of HARVEY L. BEECHER.

'You know, I'm kind of surprised you didn't draft this document yourself. You've probably forgotten more Florida probate law than I've ever learned.'

'That might be true,' the Judge says in his driest tone. 'At my age, folks tend to forget a great deal.'

Wayland flushes to the roots of his hair. 'I didn't mean –'

'I know what you mean, son,' the Judge says. 'No offence taken. Not a mite. But since you ask . . . you know that old saying about how a man who serves as his own lawyer has a fool for a client?'

Wayland grins. 'Heard it and used it plenty of times when I'm wearing my public defender hat and some sad-sack wife-abuser or hit-and-runner tells me he's going to go the DIY route in court.'

'I'm sure you have, but here's the other half: a lawyer who serves as his own lawyer has a *great* fool for a client. Goes for criminal, civil and probate law. So, shall we get down to business? Time is short.' This is something he means in more ways than one.

They get down to business. Mrs Riley has left decaf coffee, which Wayland rejects in favour of a Co'-Cola. He makes copious notes as the Judge dictates the changes in his dry courtroom voice, adjusting old bequests and adding new ones. The major new one – four million dollars – is to the Sarasota County Beach and Wildlife Preservation Society. In order to qualify, they must successfully petition the State Legislature to have a certain island just off the coast of Pelican Point declared forever wild.

'They won't have a problem getting that done,' the Judge says. 'You can handle the legal for them yourself. I'd prefer pro bono, but of course that's up to you. One trip to Tallahassee should do it. It's a little spit of a thing, nothing growing there but a few bushes. Governor Scott and his Tea Party cronies will be delighted.'

'Why's that, Judge?'

'Because the next time Beach and Preservation comes to them, begging money, they can say, "Didn't old Judge Beecher just give you four million? Get out of here, and don't let the door hit you in the ass on your way out!"'

Wayland agrees that this is probably just how it will go – Scott and his friends are all for giving if they're not the ones doing it – and the two men move on to the smaller bequests.

'Once I get a clean draft, we'll need two witnesses and a notary,' Wayland says when they've finished.

'I'll get all that done with this draft here, just to be safe,' the Judge says. 'If anything happens to me in the interim, it should stand up. There's no one to contest it; I've outlived them all.'

'A wise precaution, Judge. It would be good to take care of it tonight. I don't suppose your caretaker and housekeeper –'

'Won't be back until eight tomorrow,' Beecher says. 'But I'll make it the first order of business. Harry Staines on Vamo Road's a notary and he'll be glad to come over before he goes in to his office. He owes me a favour or six. You give that document to me, son. I'll lock it in my safe.'

'I ought to at least make a . . .' Wayland looks at the gnarled, outstretched hand and trails off. When a State Supreme Court judge (even a retired one) holds out his hand, demurrals must cease. What the hell, it's only an annotated draft, anyway, soon to be replaced by a clean version. He passes the unsigned will over and watches as Beecher rises (painfully) and swings a picture of the Florida Everglades out on a hidden hinge. The Judge enters the correct combination, making no attempt to hide the touchpad from view, and deposits the will on top of what looks to Wayland like a large and untidy heap of cash. Yikes.

'There!' Beecher says. 'All done and buttoned up! Except for the signing part, that is. How about a drink to celebrate? I have some fine single malt Scotch.'

'Well . . . I guess one wouldn't hurt.'

'It never hurt me when I was your age, although it does now, so you'll have to pardon me for not joining you. Decaf coffee and a little sweet tea are the strongest drinks I take these days. Ice?'

Wayland holds up two fingers, and Beecher adds two cubes to the drink with the slow ceremony of old age. Wayland takes a sip and high colour immediately dashes into his cheeks. It is the flush, Judge Beecher thinks, of a man who enjoys his tipple. As Wayland sets his glass down he says, 'Do you mind if I ask what the hurry is? You're all right, I take it?'

The Judge doubts if young Wayland takes it that way at all. He's not blind.

'A-country fair,' he says, see-sawing one hand in the air and sitting down with a grunt and a wince. Then, after consideration, he says, 'Do you really want to know what the hurry is?'

Wayland considers the question, and Beecher likes him for that. Then he nods.

'It has to do with that island we took care of just now. Probably never even noticed it, have you?'

'Can't say that I have.'

'Most people don't. It barely sticks out of the water. The sea turtles don't even bother with that old island. Yet it's special. Did you know my grandfather fought in the Spanish-American War?'

'No, sir, I did not.' Wayland speaks with exaggerated respect, and Beecher knows the boy believes his mind is wandering. The boy is wrong. Beecher's mind has never been clearer, and now that he's begun, he finds that he wants to tell this story at least once, before . . .

Well, before.

'Yes. There's a photograph of him standing on top of San Juan Hill. It's around here someplace. Grampy claimed to have fought in the Civil War as well, but my research – for my memoirs, you understand – proved conclusively that he couldn't have. He would have been a mere child, if born at all. But he was quite the fanciful gentleman, and he had a way of making me believe the wildest tales. Why would I not? I was only a child, not long from believing in Kris Kringle and the tooth fairy.'

'Was he a lawyer, like you and your father?'

'No, son, he was a thief. The original Light-Finger Harry. Anything that wasn't nailed down. Only like most thieves who don't get caught – our current governor might be a case in point – he called himself a businessman. His chief business – and chief thievery – was land. He bought bug- and gator-infested Florida acreage cheap and sold it dear to folks who must have been as gullible as I was as a child. Balzac once said, "Behind every great fortune there is a great crime." That's certainly true of the Beecher family, and please remember that you're my lawyer. Anything I say to you must be held in confidence.'

'Yes, Judge.' Wayland takes another sip of his drink. It is by far the finest Scotch he has ever drunk.

'Grampy Beecher was the one who pointed that island out to me.

I was ten. He had care of me for the day, and I suppose he wanted some peace and quiet. Or maybe what he wanted was a bit noisier. There was a pretty housemaid, and he may have been in hopes of investigating beneath her petticoats. So he told me that Edward Teach – better known as Blackbeard – had supposedly buried a great treasure out there. "Nobody's ever found it, Havie," he said – Havie's what he called me – "but you might be the one. A fortune in jewels and gold doubloons." You'll know what I did next.'

'I suppose you went out there and left your grandfather to cheer up the maid.'

The Judge nods, smiling. 'I took the old wooden canoe we had tied up to the dock. Went like my hair was on fire and my tail feathers were catching. Didn't take but five minutes to paddle out there. Takes me three times as long these days, and that's if the water's smooth. The island's all rock and brush on the landward side, but there's a dune of fine beach sand on the Gulf side. It never goes away. In the eighty years I've been going out there, it never seems to change. At least not geographically.'

'Didn't find any treasure, I suppose?'

'I did, in a way, but it wasn't jewels and gold. It was a name, written in the sand of that dune. As if with a stick, you know, only I didn't see any stick. The letters were drawn deep, and the sun struck shadows into them, making them stand out. Almost as if they were floating.'

'What was the name, Judge?'

'I think you have to see it written to understand.'

The Judge takes a sheet of paper from the top drawer of his desk, prints carefully, then turns the paper around so Wayland can read it: ROBIE LADOOSH.

'All right . . .' Wayland says cautiously.

'On any other day, I would have gone treasure-hunting with this very boy, because he was my best friend, and you know how boys are when they're best friends.'

'Joined at the hip,' Wayland says, smiling.

'Tight as a new key in a new lock,' Wayland agrees. 'But it was summer and he'd gone off with his parents to visit his mama's people in Virginia or Maryland or some such northern clime. So I was on my own. But attend me closely, counsellor. The boy's *actual* name was Robert LaDoucette.'

Again Wayland says, 'All right . . .' The Judge thinks that sort of leading drawl could become annoying over time, but it isn't a thing he'll ever have to actually find out, so he lets it go.

'He was my best friend and I was his, but there was a whole gang of boys we ran around with, and everyone called him Robbie LaDoosh. You follow?'

'I guess,' Wayland says, but the Judge can see he doesn't. That's understandable; Beecher has had a lot more time to think about these things. Often on sleepless nights.

'Remember that I was ten. If I had been asked to spell my friend's nickname, I would have done it just this way.' He taps ROBIE LADOOSH. Speaking almost to himself, he adds: 'So some of the magic comes from me. It *must* come from me. The question is, how much?'

'You're saying you didn't write that name in the sand?'

'No. I thought I made that clear.'

'One of your other friends, then?'

'They were all from Nokomis Village, and didn't even know about that island. We never would have paddled out to such an uninteresting little rock on our own. Robbie knew it was there, he was also from the Point, but he was hundreds of miles north.'

'All right . . .'

'My chum Robbie never came back from that vacation. We got word a week or so later that he'd taken a fall while out horseback riding. He broke his neck. Killed instantly. His parents were heartbroken. So was I, of course.'

There is silence while Wayland considers this. While they both consider it. Somewhere far off, a helicopter beats at the sky over the Gulf. The DEA looking for drug runners, the Judge supposes. He hears them every night. It's the modern age, and in some ways – in many – he'll be glad to be shed of it.

At last Wayland says, 'Are you saying what I think you're saying?'

'Well, I don't know,' the Judge says. 'What do you think I'm saying?'

But Anthony Wayland is a lawyer, and refusing to be drawn in is an ingrained habit with him. 'Did you tell your grandfather?'

'On the day the telegram about Robbie came, he wasn't there to tell. He never stayed in one place for long. We didn't see him again for six months or more. No, I kept it to myself. And like Mary after she gave birth to Jesus, I considered these things in my heart.'

'And what conclusion did you draw?'

'I kept canoeing out to that island to look at the dune, and that should answer your question. There was nothing . . . and nothing . . . and nothing. I guess I was on the verge of forgetting all about it, but then I went out one afternoon after school and there was another name written in the sand. *Printed* in the sand, to be courtroom-exact. No sign of a stick that time, either, although I suppose a stick could have been thrown into the water. This time the name was Peter Alderson. It meant nothing to me until a few days later. It was my chore to go out to the end of the road and get the paper, and it was my habit to scan the front page while I walked back up the drive – which, as you know from driving it yourself, is a good quarter-mile long. In the summer I'd also check on how the Washington Senators had done, because back then they were as close to a Southern team as we had.

'This particular day, a headline on the bottom of the front page caught my eye: WINDOW WASHER KILLED IN TRAGIC FALL. The poor guy was doing the third-floor windows of the Sarasota Public Library when the scaffolding he was standing on gave way. His name was Peter Alderson.'

The Judge can see from Wayland's face that he believes this is either a prank or some sort of elaborate fantasy the Judge is spinning out. He can also see that Wayland is enjoying his drink, and when the Judge moves to top it up, Wayland doesn't say no. And, really, the young man's belief or disbelief is beside the point. It's just such a luxury to tell it.

'Maybe you see why I go back and forth in my mind about where the magic lies,' Beecher says. 'I *knew* Robbie, and the misspelling of his name was my misspelling. But I didn't know this window washer from Adam. In any case, that's when the dune really started to get a hold on me. I began going out every day when I was here, a habit that's continued into my very old age. I respect the place, I fear the place, but most of all, I'm addicted to the place.

'Over the years, many names have appeared on that dune, and the people the names belong to always die. Sometimes it's within the week, sometimes it's two, but it's never more than a month. Some have been people I knew, and if it's by a nickname I knew them, it's the nickname I see. One day in 1940 I paddled out there and saw GRAMPY BEECHER drawn into the sand. He died in Key West three days later. Heart attack.'

With the air of someone humouring a man who is mentally unbalanced but not actually dangerous, Wayland asks, 'Did you never try to interfere with this . . . this process? Call your grandfather, for instance, and tell him to see a doctor?'

Beecher shakes his head. 'I didn't *know* it was a heart attack until we got word from the Monroe County medical examiner, did I? It could have been an accident, or even a murder. Certainly there were people who had reasons to hate my grandfather; his dealings were not of the purest sort.'

'Still . . . he was your grandfather and all . . .'

'The truth, counsellor, is that I was afraid. I felt – I still feel – as if there on that island, there's a hatch that's come ajar. On this side is what we're pleased to call "the real world". On the other is all the machinery of the universe, running at top speed. Only a fool would stick his hand into such machinery in an attempt to stop it.'

'Judge Beecher, if you want your paperwork to sail through probate, I'd keep quiet about all this. You might think there's no one to contest your will, but when large amounts of money are at stake, third and fourth cousins have a way of coming out of the woodwork. And you know the criterion: "Being of sound mind and body."'

'I've kept it to myself for eighty years,' Beecher says, and in his voice Wayland can hear *objection overruled*. 'Never a word until now. And I'm sure *you* won't talk.'

'Of course not,' Wayland says.

'I was always excited on days when names appeared in the sand – unhealthily excited, I'm sure – but terrified of the phenomenon only once. That single time I was *deeply* terrified, and fled back to the Point in my canoe as if devils were after me. Shall I tell you?'

'Please.' Wayland lifts his drink and sips. Why not? Billable hours are, after all, billable hours.

'It was 1959. I was still on the Point. I've always lived here except for the years in Tallahassee, and it's better not to speak of them . . . although I now think part of the hate I felt for that provincial backwater of a town, perhaps even most of it, was simply a masked longing for the island, and the dune. I kept wondering what I was missing, you see. *Who* I was missing. Being able to read obituaries in advance gives a man an extraordinary sense of power. Perhaps you find that unlovely. The truth often is.

'So. 1959. Harvey Beecher lawyering in Sarasota and living at Pelican Point. If it wasn't pouring down rain when I got home, I'd always change into old clothes and paddle out to the island for a look-see before supper. On this particular day I'd been kept at the office late, and by the time I'd gotten out to the island, tied up, and walked over to the dune side, the sun was going down big and red, as it so often does over the Gulf. What I saw stunned me. I literally could not move.

'There wasn't just one name written in the sand that evening but many, and in that red sunset light they looked as if they had been written in blood. They were crammed together, they wove in and out, they were written over and above and up and down. The whole length and breadth of the dune was covered with a tapestry of names. The ones down by the water had been half erased.'

Wayland looks awed in spite of his core disbelief.

'I think I screamed. I can't remember for sure, but yes, I think so. What I *do* remember is breaking the paralysis and running away as fast as I could, down the path to where my canoe was tied up. It seemed to take me forever to unpluck the knot, and when I did, I pushed the canoe out into the water before I climbed in. I was soaked from head to toe, and it's a wonder I didn't tip over. Although in those days I could have easily swum to shore, pushing the canoe ahead of me. Not these days; if I tipped my kayak over now, that would be all, she wrote.'

'Then I suggest you stay onshore, at least until your will is signed, witnessed and notarized.'

Judge Beecher gives the young man a wintry smile. 'You needn't worry about that, son,' he says. He looks toward the window, and the Gulf beyond. His face is long and thoughtful. 'Those names . . . I can see them yet, jostling each other for place on that blood-red dune. Two days later, a TWA plane on its way to Miami crashed in the Glades. All one hundred and nineteen souls on board were killed. The passenger list was in the paper. I recognized some of the names. I recognized *many* of them.'

'You *saw* this. You saw those names.'

'Yes. For several months after that I stayed away from the island, and I promised myself I would stay away for good. I suppose drug addicts make the same promises to themselves about their dope, don't they? And like them, I eventually weakened and resumed my old habit. Now, counsellor: do you understand why I called you out here to finish the work on my will, and why it had to be tonight?'

Wayland doesn't believe a word of it, but like many fantasies, this one has its own internal logic. It's easy enough to follow. The Judge is ninety, his once ruddy complexion has gone the colour of clay, his formerly firm step has become shuffling and tentative. He's clearly in pain, and he's lost weight he can't afford to lose.

'I suppose that today you saw your name in the sand,' Wayland says.

Judge Beecher looks momentarily startled, and then he smiles. It is a terrible smile, transforming his narrow, pallid face into a death's-head grin.

'Oh no,' he says. 'Not *mine*.' ■

DIEM PERDIDI

Julie Otsuka

She remembers her name. She remembers the name of the president. She remembers the name of the president's dog. She remembers what city she lives in. And on which street. And in which house. *The one with the big olive tree where the road takes a turn.* She remembers what year it is. She remembers the season. She remembers the day on which you were born. She remembers the daughter who was born before you – *She had your father's nose, that was the first thing I noticed about her* – but she does not remember that daughter's name. She remembers the name of the man she did not marry – Frank – and she keeps his letters in a drawer by her bed. She remembers that you once had a husband, but she refuses to remember your ex-husband's name. *That man,* she calls him.

She does not remember how she got the bruises on her arms or going for a walk with you earlier this morning. She does not remember bending over, during that walk, and plucking a flower from a neighbour's front yard and slipping it into her hair. *Maybe your father will kiss me now.* She does not remember what she ate for dinner last night, or when she last took her medicine. She does not remember to drink enough water. She does not remember to comb her hair.

She remembers the rows of dried persimmons that once hung from the eaves of her mother's house in Berkeley. *They were the most beautiful shade of orange.* She remembers that your father loves peaches. She remembers that every Sunday morning, at ten, he takes her for a drive down to the sea in the brown car. She remembers that every evening, right before the eight o'clock news, he sets out two fortune cookies on a paper plate and announces to her that they are having a party. She remembers that on Mondays he comes home from the college at four, and if he is even five minutes late she goes out to the gate and begins to wait for him. She remembers which bedroom is hers and which is his. She remembers that the bedroom that is now hers was once yours. She remembers that it wasn't always like this.

She remembers the first line of the song, 'How High the Moon'. She remembers the Pledge of Allegiance. She remembers her Social Security number. She remembers her best friend Jean's telephone number even though Jean has been dead for six years. She remembers that Margaret is dead. She remembers that Betty is dead. She remembers that Grace has stopped calling. She remembers that her own mother died nine years ago, while spading the soil in her garden, and she misses her more and more every day. *It doesn't go away.* She remembers the number assigned to her family by the government right after the start of the war. *13611.* She remembers being sent away to the desert with her mother and brother during the fifth month of that war and taking her first ride on a train. She remembers the day they came home. *September 9, 1945.* She remembers the sound of the wind hissing through the sagebrush. She remembers the scorpions and red ants. She remembers the taste of dust.

Whenever you stop by to see her she remembers to give you a big hug, and you are always surprised at her strength. She remembers to give you a kiss every time you leave. She remembers to tell you, at the end of every phone call, that the FBI will check up on you again soon. She remembers to ask you if you would like her to iron your blouse for you before you go out on a date. She remembers to smooth down your skirt. *Don't give it all away.* She remembers to brush aside a wayward strand of your hair. She does not remember eating lunch with you twenty minutes ago and suggests that you go out to Marie Callender's for sandwiches and pie. She does not remember that she herself once used to make the most beautiful pies with perfectly fluted crusts. She does not remember how to iron your blouse for you or when she began to forget. *Something's changed.* She does not remember what she is supposed to do next.

She remembers that the daughter who was born before you lived for half an hour and then died. *She looked perfect from the outside.* She remembers her mother telling her, more than once, *Don't you ever let anyone see you cry.* She remembers giving you your first bath on your third day in the world. She remembers that you were a very fat baby. She remembers that your first word was *No.* She remembers picking apples in a field with Frank many years ago in the rain. *It was the best day of my life.* She remembers that the first time she met him she was so nervous she forgot her own address. She remembers wearing too much lipstick. She remembers not sleeping for days.

When you drive past Hesse Park, she remembers being asked to leave her exercise class by her teacher after being in that class for more than ten years. *I shouldn't have talked so much.* She remembers touching her toes and doing windmills and jumping jacks on the freshly mown grass. She remembers being the highest kicker in her class. She does not remember how to use the 'new' coffee maker, which is now three years old, because it was bought after she began to forget. She does not remember asking your father, ten minutes ago, if today is Sunday, or if it is time to go for her ride. She does not remember where she last put her sweater or how long she has been sitting in her chair. She does not always remember how to get out of that chair, and so you gently push down on the footrest and offer her your hand, which she does not always remember to take. *Go away,* she sometimes says. Other times, she just says, *I'm stuck.* She does not remember saying to you, the other night, right after your father left the room, *He loves me more than I love him.* She does not remember saying to you, a moment later, *I can hardly wait until he comes back.*

She remembers that when your father was courting her he was always on time. She remembers thinking that he had a nice smile. *He still does.* She remembers that when they first met he was engaged to another woman. She remembers that that other woman was white. She remembers that that other woman's parents did not want their daughter to marry a man who looked like the gardener. She remembers that the winters were colder back then, and that there were days on which you actually had to put on a coat and scarf. She remembers her mother bowing her head every morning at the altar and offering her ancestors a bowl of hot rice. She remembers the smell of incense and pickled cabbage in the kitchen. She remembers that her father always wore nice shoes. She remembers that the night the FBI came for him, he and her mother had just had another big fight. She remembers not seeing him again until after the end of the war.

She does not always remember to trim her toenails, and when you soak her feet in the bucket of warm water she closes her eyes and leans back in her chair and reaches out for your hand. *Don't give up on me.* She does not remember how to tie her shoelaces, or fasten the hooks on her bra. She does not remember that she has been wearing her favourite blue blouse for five days in a row. She does not remember your age. *Just wait till you have children of your own,* she says to you, even though you are now too old to do so.

She remembers that after the first girl was born and then died, she sat in the yard for days, just staring at the roses by the pond. *I didn't know what else to do.* She remembers that when you were born you, too, had your father's long nose. *It was as if I'd given birth to the same girl twice.* She remembers that you are a Taurus. She remembers that your birthstone is green. She remembers to read you your horoscope from the newspaper whenever you come over to see her. *Someone you were once very close to may soon reappear in your life.* She does not remember reading you that same horoscope five minutes ago or going to the doctor with you last week after you discovered a bump on the back of her head. *I think I fell.* She does not remember telling the doctor that you are no longer married, or giving him your number and asking him to please call. She does not remember leaning over and whispering to you, the moment he stepped out of the room, *I think he'll do.*

She remembers another doctor asking her, fifty years ago, minutes after the first girl was born and then died, if she wanted to donate the baby's body to science. *He said she had a very unusual heart.* She remembers being in labour for thirty-two hours. She remembers being too tired to think. *So I told him yes.* She remembers driving home from the hospital in the sky-blue Chevy with your father and neither one of them saying a word. She remembers knowing she'd made a big mistake. She does not remember what happened to the baby's body and worries that it might be stuck in a jar. She does not remember why they didn't just bury her. *I wish she were under a tree.* She remembers wanting to bring her flowers every day.

She remembers that even as a young girl you said you did not want to have children. She remembers that you hated wearing dresses. She remembers that you never played with dolls. She remembers that the first time you bled you were thirteen years old and wearing bright yellow pants. She remembers that your childhood dog was named Shiro. She remembers that you once had a cat named Gasoline. She remembers that you had two turtles named Turtle. She remembers that the first time she and your father took you to Japan to meet his family you were eighteen months old and just beginning to speak. She remembers leaving you with his mother in the tiny silkworm village in the mountains while she and your father travelled across the island for ten days. *I worried about you the whole time.* She remembers that when they came back you did not know who she was and that for many days afterwards you would not speak to her, you would only whisper in her ear.

She remembers that the year you turned five you refused to leave the house without tapping the door frame three times. She remembers that you had a habit of clicking your teeth repeatedly, which drove her up the wall. She remembers that you could not stand it when different-coloured foods were touching on the plate. *Everything had to be just so.* She remembers trying to teach you to read before you were ready. She remembers taking you to Newberry's to pick out patterns and fabric and teaching you how to sew. She remembers that every night, after dinner, you would sit down next to her at the kitchen table and hand her the bobby pins one by one as she set the curlers in her hair. She remembers that this was her favourite part of the day. *I wanted to be with you all the time.*

She remembers that you were conceived on the first try. She remembers that your brother was conceived on the first try. She remembers that your other brother was conceived on the second try. *We must not have been paying attention.* She remembers that a palm reader once told her that she would never be able to bear children because her uterus was tipped the wrong way. She remembers that a blind fortune-teller once told her that she had been a man in her past life, and that Frank had been her sister. She remembers that everything she remembers is not necessarily true. She remembers the horse-drawn garbage carts on Ashby, her first pair of crepe-soled shoes, scattered flowers by the side of the road. She remembers that the sound of Frank's voice always made her feel calmer. She remembers that every time they parted he turned around and watched her walk away. She remembers that the first time he asked her to marry him she told him she wasn't ready. She remembers that the second time she said she wanted to wait until she was finished with school. She remembers walking along the water with him one warm summer evening on the boardwalk and being so happy she could not remember her own name. She remembers not knowing that it wouldn't be like this with any of the others. She remembers thinking she had all the time in the world.

She does not remember the names of the flowers in the yard whose names she has known for years. *Roses? Daffodils? Immortelles?* She does not remember that today is Sunday, and she has already gone for her ride. She does not remember to call you, even though she always says that she will. She remembers how to play 'Clair de Lune' on the piano. She remembers how to play 'Chopsticks' and scales. She remembers not to talk to telemarketers when they call on the telephone. *We're not interested.* She remembers her grammar. *Just between you and me.* She remembers her manners. She remembers to say thank you and please. She remembers to wipe herself every time she uses the toilet. She remembers to flush. She remembers to turn her wedding ring around whenever she pulls on her silk stockings. She remembers to reapply her lipstick every time she leaves the house. She remembers to put on her anti-wrinkle cream every night before climbing into bed. *It works while you sleep.* In the morning, when she wakes, she remembers her dreams. *I was walking through a forest. I was swimming in a river. I was looking for Frank in a city I did not know and no one would tell me where he was.*

On Halloween day, she remembers to ask you if you are going out trick-or-treating. She remembers that your father hates pumpkin. *It's all he ate in Japan during the war.* She remembers listening to him pray, every night, when they first got married, that he would be the one to die first. She remembers playing marbles on a dirt floor in the desert with her brother and listening to the couple at night on the other side of the wall. *They were at it all the time.* She remembers the box of chocolates you brought back to her after your honeymoon in Paris. 'But will it last?' you asked her. She remembers her own mother telling her, 'The moment you fall in love with someone, you are lost.'

She remembers that when her father came back after the war he and her mother fought even more than they had before. She remembers that he would spend entire days shopping for shoes in

San Francisco while her mother scrubbed other people's floors. She remembers that some nights he would walk around the block three times before coming into the house. She remembers that one night he did not come in at all. She remembers that when your own husband left you, five years ago, you broke out in hives all over your body for weeks. She remembers thinking he was trouble the moment she met him. *A mother knows.* She remembers keeping that thought to herself. *I had to let you make your own mistakes.*

She remembers that, of her three children, you were the most delightful to be with. She remembers that your younger brother was so quiet she sometimes forgot he was there. *He was like a dream.* She remembers that her own brother refused to carry anything with him on to the train except for his rubber toy truck. *He wouldn't let me touch it.* She remembers her mother killing all the chickens in the yard the day before they left. She remembers her fifth-grade teacher, Mr Martello, asking her to stand up in front of the class so everyone could tell her goodbye. She remembers being given a silver heart pendant by her next-door neighbour, Elaine Crowley, who promised to write but never did. She remembers losing that pendant on the train and being so angry she wanted to cry. *It was my first piece of jewellery.*

She remembers that one month after Frank joined the Air Force he suddenly stopped writing her letters. She remembers worrying that he'd been shot down over Korea or taken hostage by guerrillas in the jungle. She remembers thinking about him every minute of the day. *I thought I was losing my mind.* She remembers learning from a friend one night that he had fallen in love with somebody else. She remembers asking your father the next day to marry her. *'Shall we go get the ring?' I said to him.* She remembers telling him, *'It's time.'*

When you take her to the supermarket she remembers that coffee is Aisle Two. She remembers that Aisle Three is milk. She remembers the name of the cashier in the express lane who always gives her a big hug. *Diane.* She remembers the name of the girl at the flower stand who always gives her a single broken-stemmed rose. She remembers that the man behind the meat counter is Big Lou. 'Well, hello, gorgeous,' he says to her. She does not remember where her purse is, and begins to panic until you remind her that she has left it at home. *I don't feel like myself without it.* She does not remember asking the man in line behind her whether or not he was married. She does not remember him telling her, rudely, that he was not. She does not remember staring at the old woman in the wheelchair by the melons and whispering to you, *I hope I never end up like that.* She remembers that the huge mimosa tree that once stood next to the cart corral in the parking lot is no longer there. *Nothing stays the same.* She remembers that she was once a very good driver. She remembers failing her last driver's test three times in a row. *I couldn't remember any of the rules.* She remembers that the day after her father left them her mother sprinkled little piles of salt in the corner of every room to purify the house. She remembers that they never spoke of him again.

She does not remember asking your father, when he comes home from the pharmacy, what took him so long, or whom he talked to, or whether or not the pharmacist was pretty. She does not always remember his name. She remembers graduating from high school with high honours in Latin. She remembers how to say, 'I came, I saw, I conquered.' *Veni, vidi, vici.* She remembers how to say, 'I have lost the day.' *Diem perdidi.* She remembers the words for 'I'm sorry' in Japanese, which you have not heard her utter in years. She remembers the words for 'rice' and 'toilet'. She remembers the words for 'Wait'. *Chotto matte kudasai.* She remembers that a white-snake dream will bring you good luck. She remembers that it is bad luck to pick up a dropped comb. She remembers that you should never run to a funeral. She remembers that you shout the truth down into a well.

She remembers going to work, like her mother, for the rich white ladies up in the hills. She remembers Mrs Tindall, who insisted on eating lunch with her every day in the kitchen instead of just leaving her alone. She remembers Mrs Edward deVries, who fired her after one day. *'Who taught you how to iron?' she asked me.* She remembers that Mrs Cavanaugh would not let her go home on Saturdays until she had baked an apple pie. She remembers Mrs Cavanaugh's husband, Arthur, who liked to put his hand on her knee. She remembers that he sometimes gave her money. She remembers that she never refused. She remembers once stealing a silver candlestick from a cupboard but she cannot remember whose it was. She remembers that they never missed it. She remembers using the same napkin for three days in a row. She remembers that today is Sunday, which six days out of seven is not true.

When you bring home the man you hope will become your next husband, she remembers to take his jacket. She remembers to offer him coffee. She remembers to offer him cake. She remembers to thank him for the roses. *So you like her?* she asks him. She remembers to ask him his name. *She's my first-born, you know.* She remembers, five minutes later, that she has already forgotten his name, and asks him again what it is. *That's my brother's name,* she tells him. She does not remember talking to her brother on the phone earlier that morning – *He promised me he'd call* – or going for a walk with you in the park. She does not remember how to make coffee. She does not remember how to serve cake.

She remembers sitting next to her brother many years ago on a train to the desert and fighting about who got to lie down on the seat. She remembers hot white sand, the wind on the water, someone's voice telling her, *Hush, it's all right.* She remembers where she was the day the men landed on the moon. She remembers the day they learned that Japan had lost the war. *It was the only time I ever saw my mother cry.* She remembers the day she learned that Frank had married somebody else. *I read about it in the paper.* She remembers the letter she got from him not long after, asking if he could please see her. *He said he'd made a mistake.* She remembers writing him back, 'It's too late.' She remembers marrying your father on an unusually warm day in December. She remembers having their first fight, three months later, in March. *I threw a chair.* She remembers that he comes home from the college every Monday at four. She remembers that she is forgetting. She remembers less and less every day.

When you ask her your name, she does not remember what it is. *Ask your father. He'll know.* She does not remember the name of the president. She does not remember the name of the president's dog. She does not remember the season. She does not remember the day or the year. She remembers the little house on San Luis Avenue that she first lived in with your father. She remembers her mother leaning over the bed she once shared with her brother and kissing the two of them goodnight. She remembers that as soon as the first girl was born she knew that something was wrong. *She didn't cry.* She remembers holding the baby in her arms and watching her go to sleep for the first and last time in her life. She remembers that they never buried her. She remembers that they did not give her a name. She remembers that the baby had perfect fingernails and a very unusual heart. She remembers that she had your father's long nose. She remembers knowing at once that she was his. She remembers beginning to bleed two days later when she came home from the hospital. She remembers your father catching her in the bathroom as she began to fall. She remembers a desert sky at sunset. *It was the most beautiful shade of orange.* She remembers scorpions and red ants. She remembers the taste of dust. She remembers once loving someone more than anyone else. She remembers giving birth to the same girl twice. She remembers that today is Sunday, and it is time to go for her ride, and so she picks up her purse and puts on her lipstick and goes out to wait for your father in the car. ∎

ABOUT THE COVER

Jake & Dinos Chapman

As evening falls, I sit at my desk – the gibbous moon at my shoulder, flooding the studio with its wan light – to draw, to meditate on the beauty of God's creation and the wonders therein. Yet, as ever, my attempts are mocked by the monstrosities that leer up at me from the page, wrenching me from my reverie, leaving me able only to stare aghast at the horrors that materialize and multiply before my eyes, seeping unbidden, crowding at the edges of my vision as if from a foul universe beyond the very fibres of the parchment, drawn forth by the frenzied scuttling dance of my accursed hand across the sheet, in its insane labour to describe and catalogue its most vile, degenerate subjects. Each infinitesimal imperfection of the virgin surface seized upon, worried at, amplified and distorted, now becoming a gaping slathering maw, foul pulsating tendrils, ravaged, bloated, heaving flesh or sightless rheumy eyes, staring blankly past me into the vast emptiness of the night.

I am seized, transfixed in this manner. Immobile. Hour upon unremitting hour, hostage to the unsolicited action of my traitorous hand. A vast lexicon of filth spreading seamlessly across innumerable sheets that, upon completion, fall to the floor, the next sheet already snatched up to commence anew, again and again, until I eventually fall unconscious, spent, bled dry. As the weak sun rises, my limbs once again my own, I crawl to my bed.

I cannot, nor do I wish to, lay claim to any of these nocturnal flights. I cannot explain why they occur, nor can I imagine how to thwart their malign progress. The moon drags me nightly to my desk. Seemingly it has purpose, of this I am sure. But I cannot guess. I do not know when my task will be complete, if it will ever be done. I grow weaker with each session, and the moon's lustre gleams colder each night . . . ∎

254

CONTRIBUTORS

Daniel Alarcón's *Lost City Radio* won the International Literature Prize in 2009. He is founder of Radio Ambulante, a Spanish-language storytelling podcast.

Chris Andrews's translation of Roberto Bolaño's *Distant Star* won the Valle Inclán Prize in 2005. He teaches at the University of Western Sydney in Australia.

Paul Auster is the author of *The Book of Illusions, The Brooklyn Follies, The New York Trilogy* and *The Invention of Solitude*. 'Your Birthday Has Come and Gone' is an extract from his forthcoming memoir, *Winter Journal* (A Frances Coady Book, Henry Holt/Faber).

Tom Bamforth has worked with humanitarian organizations in Pakistan, Sudan and the Pacific.

Roberto Bolaño (1953–2003) won the National Book Critics Circle Award for his novel *2666*. *Between Parentheses*, a collection of writings, was published in 2011.

Don DeLillo has written fifteen novels and three stage plays. 'The Starveling' will appear in *The Angel Esmeralda: Nine Stories*, forthcoming in 2011 from Scribner/Picador.

Mark Doty's *Fire to Fire: New and Selected Poems* won the National Book Award for Poetry. He is at work on a prose volume on Walt Whitman, sex, death and the body.

Sarah Hall's 'She Murdered Mortal He' is taken from her first story collection, *The Beautiful Indifference*, to be published by Faber & Faber in November 2011.

Stephen King is the author of more than fifty books. His next is a novel, *11/22/63*, published in November 2011.

Alfred Mac Adam is professor of Latin American literature at Barnard College–Columbia University. His most recent translation is *Season of Ash* by Jorge Volpi.

Kanitta Meechubot graduated from Central Saint Martins College with an MA in Communication Design (Illustration) in 2011.

Julie Otsuka is the author of *When the Emperor Was Divine*. Her second novel, *The Buddha in the Attic*, was published this year.

Rajesh Parameswaran's first story collection, *I Am an Executioner: Love Stories*, is forthcoming from Knopf and Bloomsbury in 2012.

D.A. Powell's books include *Cocktails* and *Chronic*. A 2011 Guggenheim Fellow, Powell teaches at the University of San Francisco.

Santiago Roncagliolo's *Red April* won the 2011 Independent Foreign Fiction Prize. His books have been translated into fifteen languages and he was named one of *Granta*'s Best Young Spanish-Language Novelists in 2010.

Will Self is the acclaimed author of numerous books, both fiction and non-fiction. His website is will-self.com.

Joy Williams has written four novels, three story collections, and *Ill Nature*, a book of essays. She was inducted into the American Academy of Arts and Letters in 2008.

GRANTA 117: AUTUMN 2011 | EVENTS

UK

The Shining Path: Santiago Roncagliolo and Oscar Guardiola-Rivera in conversation
31 October. Details tbc
The brutal tactics of the Shining Path, a Maoist guerrilla organization, widely affected the people of Peru. In his essay for *Granta* 117, Santiago Roncagliolo recalls how his childhood was shaped by the Shining Path and investigates the aftermath of terror on the country – and on the insurgents themselves. Roncagliolo is a *Granta* Best Young Spanish-Language Novelist and winner of the Independent Foreign Fiction Prize for the novel *Red April*.

Tales of Terror
1 November, doors open at 6 p.m., event starts at 7 p.m., The Last Tuesday Society, 11 Mare Street, London E8 4RP
Join us for an evening of chilling tales and a chance to explore the macabre curiosities at Viktor Wynd's little shop of horrors. Enjoy dramatic readings of a never-before-heard story by Stephen King and other pieces from *Granta* 117: Horror. In association with the Hendrick's Lecture Series and Liars' League. Please visit www.thelasttuesdaysociety.org for ticket information. Each ticket includes a copy of the magazine.

Granta 117: Horror, London Launch
2 November, 6.30 p.m., Foyles, 113–119 Charing Cross Road, London WC2H 0EB
Mark Doty discusses the unexpected relationship between Bram Stoker and Walt Whitman. Will Self recounts the horror of blood-letting.

An Evening with Mark Doty
3 November, 7 p.m., Gay's the Word, 66 Marchmont Street, London WC1N 1AB
Mark Doty explores the nature of blood, Bram Stoker and Walt Whitman through reading and conversation.

Visions of Horror: A Salon
Details tbc, The Hospital Club, 24 Endell Street, London WC2H 9HQ
What creates horror? Join *Granta* and the Hospital Club to mark the launch of the new issue, with a focus on art and design. Special guests to be announced. Ticket details tbc.

Granta 117: Horror, Nottingham Launch
1 November, 7 p.m., Waterstone's, 1–5 Bridlesmith Gate, Nottingham NG1 2GR. Tickets from £3
Santiago Roncagliolo hosts a celebration with readings and discussion to mark the launch of *Granta* 117. Contact the store for ticket information on tel: 0843 290 8525.

USA

The Housing Works Horror Halloween Party
31 October, 7 p.m., Housing Works Bookstore, 126 Crosby Street, New York, NY 10012
A Halloween party with tricks and treats for the literary set, including readings from Julie Otsuka, Rajesh Parameswaran and others.

Granta 117: Horror, Brooklyn
1 November, 7 p.m., Greenlight Bookstore, 686 Fulton Street, Brooklyn, NY 11217
To celebrate the launch of *Granta* 117, emerging author Rajesh Parameswaran and others plumb the depths of horror and discuss their stories from the magazine.

Granta 117: Horror, Manhattan
29 November, 7 p.m., Barnes and Noble, 33 East 17th Street, New York, NY 10003
Paul Auster and Don DeLillo discuss their new work in *Granta* 117 and explore the horrors of everyday life.

Granta 117: Horror, San Francisco
3 November, Green Apple Books, 506 Clement Street, San Francisco, CA 94118.
D.A. Powell hosts an evening of readings and conversation.